Transforming
HEALTH CARE PHILANTHROPY

Transforming
HEALTH CARE PHILANTHROPY

EDITOR BETSY CHAPIN TAYLOR

For permission requests, please address
Association for Healthcare Philanrthopy
313 Park Ave., Suite 400
Falls Church, VA 22046
Email: ahp@ahp.org

Published 2017 by Association for Healthcare Philanthropy Press
Printed in the United States of America

1 2 3 4 5 6 7 8 9 10.

ISBN 978-0-692-92124-1

This book is dedicated to all those who advance the field of health care philanthropy for the purpose, passion and unflagging dedication you bring to this noble work.

Table of Contents

i

About the Authors

Christopher M. Cannon, CFRE

Chris Cannon is a thought leader in fund development operations. As the president of strategic services for Zuri Group, he shapes how organizations optimize data, reporting, technology, processes and people. Prior to launching Zuri's strategic services unit, he provided counsel as a managing associate with Bentz Whaley Flessner. A seasoned fundraising professional with two decades of experience, Cannon has also held campaign and organizational leadership roles at Saint Louis University and Saint Louis Zoo. Cannon authored *An Executive's Guide to Fundraising Operations* to help professionals leverage operations to raise more money.

David Collis

David Collis is president of Florida Hospital Foundation; he assumed this role in 2009. Collis works in partnership with ten foundation boards which recently completed a $150 million comprehensive campaign which surpassed goal with $154 million. Collis has spent more than 20 years in development at organizations including Georgetown University Cuba Project and at Rollins College for a campaign which ended with more than $160 million in commitments. He has provided consulting to clients including Florida Hospital, Harbor Branch Oceanographic Institute, The Amazon Conservation Team, The Adult Literacy League and Habitat for Humanity Orlando. Collis graduated cum laude with an honors Bachelor of Arts from Rollins College and a master's degree from Georgetown University.

Amy Grenzebach Day

Amy Day is regional vice president for advancement at Loyola University Health System, overseeing philanthropy for Trinity Health Illinois as well as Loyola University Chicago Health Science Division including Stritch School of Medicine and Marcella Niehoff School of Nursing. Amy has served in leadership positions in health care philanthropy for 20 years including Ann and Robert H. Lurie Children's Hospital and Presence Health. Amy served on the Association for Healthcare Philanthropy's (AHP) strategic planning team and regularly presents at AHP conferences. Amy loves building a farm team of gift advisors and is also an avid Chicago Cubs fan.

Susan Dolbert, Ph.D.

Susan Dolbert is president and chief development officer of the Los Angeles Region of Providence St. Joseph Health. In this role, she is responsible for development at five hospitals and a hospice and palliative care home health organization. Prior to her work at Providence, she served as chief development officer for Rutgers Biomedical and Health Sciences, Fred Hutchinson Cancer Research Center and Mayo Clinic in Arizona. Dolbert is a Phi Beta Kappa graduate of Arizona State University, where she received a Bachelor of Arts degree in Political Science. She also holds a Master of Arts degree in organizational communication and a Ph.D. in Public Administration, which focused on public policy and organizational development. Both advanced degrees are also from Arizona State University.

Amy Dorrill, FAHP, CFRE

Amy Dorrill is the associate dean for development and alumni relations at Emory University's Nell Hodgson Woodruff School of Nursing, raising $27.4M in a $1.6B comprehensive campaign. Dorrill is the former chief development officer for University Health Care System, a 580+ bed Magnet Hospital, in Augusta, Georgia. Amy holds a Master of Business Administration from University of Georgia's Terry College of Business. She is a Fellow of the Association for Healthcare Philanthropy and Certified Fund Raising Executive. She was named one of Georgia Trend's Forty under Forty, the Outstanding Young Alumnus at Augusta State University and awarded the Spirit of Emory award. She has served in regional and national roles with the Association for Healthcare Philanthropy.

Fred Najjar

Fred Najjar serves as senior vice president of philanthropy for Dignity Health, one of the nation's largest health systems. Fred oversees 31 fundraising foundations including the system-wide Dignity Health Foundation. He provides vision, leadership and direction to ensure philanthropic support of programs and services for Dignity Health at the system level and for the philanthropic activities of all Dignity Health fundraising foundations. He also plays a consultative role in the hiring, training and development of leadership in the foundations, all while sharing best practices throughout the system. A native of Virginia, he holds an undergraduate degree in public administration and a graduate degree in counseling and student personnel administration, both from Virginia Tech University. He has completed coursework towards a doctorate in organization and leadership at the University of San Francisco.

Steven A. Rum

Steve Rum is vice president for development and alumni relations for the Fund for Johns Hopkins Medicine. He oversees a staff of 147 employees and a budget of more than $23 million. Since Rum's arrival at Hopkins in 2005, annual funds raised have increased steadily to $313.8 million in FY 2013; total gifts and pledges have averaged $300 million per year, with a peak in FY 2008 of $425 million. Rum is known for his success in leadership philanthropy. Under his direction, the Fund for Johns Hopkins Medicine raised $375 million for Sheikh Zayed Tower and the Bloomberg Children's Center; he personally closed a $100 million gift which enabled creation of the Brain Science Institute in the Johns Hopkins School of Medicine. Rum earned his bachelor's degree from Georgia Southern University and his master's degree in administration from Ohio University.

Betsy Chapin Taylor, FAHP

Betsy Taylor is president of the health care philanthropy consulting firm Accordant Philanthropy. She is author of the book *Healthcare Philanthropy: Advance Charitable Giving to Your Organization's Mission*, author of the American Hospital Association monograph *Boards and Philanthropy: Developing the Next-Curve Revenue Source for Health Care* and editor and co-author of the book *Redefining Healthcare Philanthropy*. Her work has also been featured in national trade publications including *Healthcare Executive, Trustee, H&HN Daily, The Chronicle of Philanthropy, Healthcare Philanthropy, Chief Executive Officer* and more. Taylor holds an M.B.A. from the University of Georgia and an MS of Journalism from Columbia University in New York. She is a Fellow of the Association for Healthcare Philanthropy.

R. Edward Thompson, Ed.D., FCEP

Eddie Thompson founded Thompson & Associates and provides leadership and direction to more than 35 seasoned charitable estate planners as the organization's CEO. Thompson has planned thousands of estates, which have generated more than two billion dollars to charity during his thirty plus years working with nonprofits. In 1983, Thompson obtained his Doctor of Education in Higher Education Administration from Vanderbilt University. His doctoral dissertation was on successful fund development methods. His academic achievements include two M.A. degrees and a B.A. and Associate of Fine Arts. He was recognized by the National Society of Fund Raising Executives as a Certified Fund Raising Executive from 1986 to 1996. In March 2013, he was appointed to Partnership for Philanthropic Planning's Leadership Institute.

Ann Thompson-Haas, FAHP

Ann Thompson-Haas is principal of the fund development and management consulting firm Larkwood Consulting, LLC. She has more than 25 years experience in philanthropy, strategy development, organizational transformation and talent development. She previously held senior leadership positions in major health care systems, led comprehensive fund development programs and secured significant major gifts as part of $100 million+ campaigns. Thompson-Haas has taught for more than 25 years at the AHP Institute for Healthcare Philanthropy. She also taught at the Fundraising Institute of Australia's resident education program for a decade and served as editor of the AHP Advanced Course in Healthcare Philanthropy. In 2009, she was honored with AHP's Harold J. "Si" Seymour Award. Thompson-Haas holds an M.B.A. and an M.A. in Organizational Communication and is a Fellow of AHP.

Foreword

We are at a critical juncture in the field of health care fund development. Across the globe, philanthropy professionals are confronting changing demographics, changing technology and changing communication. 2017 is the Association for Healthcare Philanthropy's 50th anniversary--a time for us both to reflect on industry changes over the past five decades and to plan for the future.

AHP is committed to driving thought leadership as our field evolves now and for decades to come. We will continue to inspire, educate and serve those who advance the important work of hospitals, hospices and health systems. Your mission is our mission, and we will provide forward-thinking resources as you seek to fulfill your organizations' goals.

Transforming Health Care Philanthropy furthers our vision of becoming the definitive authority in health philanthropy. We are pleased to feature insight from thought leaders in the field, each of whom have focused on both how traditional core strategies are changing in today's environment and how the industry must explore new priorities--such as engaging key institutional allies, harnessing the power of grateful patient giving, developing agile organizations that use the latest information technology and maximizing the institutional impact of charitable funds.

I extend my deepest thanks to Betsy Chapin Taylor, FAHP, who shepherded both this project and the first book in this series, *Redefining Health Care Philanthropy*. Her expertise in the field has empowered and advanced numerous organizations over the years, and it shines through once again in this collection. I would also like to thank each author for their commitment to AHP; their generously donated time and thought leadership will benefit the entire field of philanthropy.

Steven W. Churchill, MNA
President & CEO
Association for Healthcare Philanthropy
September 2017

Preface

The moment has arrived for health care philanthropy organizations to reexamine our priorities and our methods. Our missions are too important to forgive or to ignore underperformance. Our potential is too great to be complacent about the need to change, to improve and to grow. Yet, too many organizations still cling to traditional fund development approaches that served well in another era but that fail to meet the demands of today's health care organizations and today's donor partners.

Our field must always be guided by a deep and respectful understanding of philanthropy as a noble and intrinsically-motivated benevolence toward humankind. Philanthropy professionals catalyze potential through values-based partnerships that connect donors to meaningful opportunities to achieve social impact. Values, integrity, purpose and gratitude are always the rich core of this work. Embracing a values-driven approach with a deep understanding of these commitments will make your work more rewarding, successful and meaningful.

To fulfill the potential of our calling, we must have the courage to abandon programs and approaches that no longer serve the mission well and have the conviction to forge new paths forward that infuse our work with intention, diligence and deliberateness. Every choice we make is simultaneously a choice not to do something else, so we must refine our focus and direct our resources to advance programs and partnerships that promise to be most fruitful. We must bring rigor to our work through agile use of data, processes and measurement. We must empower, enable and inspire advocates—from clinicians to executives to board members to philanthropy colleagues-to vibrantly do their part. We must rethink how we refine, reposition and maximize efforts from annual giving to planned giving. We must avidly pursue championing emerging funding priorities like population health. We must be unabashed in educating our organizations about the power of gratitude to not only transform the care experience but also philanthropy.

This book brings together inspiring and challenging thinkers from across our profession to explore opportunities to refine and enhance our shared work, but only you can make your work more relevant and more impactful. Now, you must shape your vision and summon your conviction to transform health care philanthropy.

Betsy Chapin Taylor, FAHP
Ponte Vedra Beach, FL
September 2017

Acknowledgements

This book would not have happened without the significant contributions of many.

Thank you first and foremost to the authors for championing a chapter and sharing your thought leadership with all of us. Your volunteer leadership makes a difference in moving the field and made it possible for 100% of the proceeds from this book to benefit the mission of the Association for Healthcare Philanthropy.

Thank you to the leadership, board of directors and staff of the Association for Healthcare Philanthropy for your service to all the philanthropy professionals in the field and for supporting the continued expansion of knowledge and innovation in the field of health care philanthropy. I am honored that you decided to entrust me with this book.

Thank you to my esteemed and cherished colleagues at Accordant Philanthropy for making it possible for me to take on the editing and writing of this book in the midst of all the wonderful work that we are privileged to have on our plates. Particular thanks to my colleagues Michael J. Beall for designing the cover, Avery Dayton for incredible patience and precision doing the layout and building all the graphics (it looks great!) and to Taylor Strasser for getting a jumble of citations and references into good order.

Thanks to my family for their continued support, patience, good humor and occasional tolerance of frozen food as I pursue my passion to advance this amazing field of philanthropy and to support those who are called to serve.

Thanks, finally, to all of you in the field who advance this noble work each day. You are the catalysts and conduits to enable donors to accomplish the good they have in mind. Your work facilitates the power of philanthropy to transform care and to touch lives in countless communities. It's pretty amazing.

Betsy Chapin Taylor, FAHP

CHAPTER 1

Embracing the Science Behind Grateful Engagement

Betsy Chapin Taylor, FAHP

Most health care organizations seek to proactively cultivate and recognize gratitude in patients and families with the objective to direct expressions of gratitude toward charitable giving to financially support the mission. Yet, many organizations still have a limited understanding of what "gratitude" really is. For health care organizations to create vibrant partnerships with patients and family members who are grateful, it is time for the field to usher in a deeper understanding of the psychology and science behind gratitude to advance thoughtful, respectful, integrity-based collaborations with patients and families who are moved and motivated to participate in health care philanthropy.

CAPTURING THE ESSENCE OF GRATITUDE

Throughout history, gratitude is revered in both philosophy and various religious traditions as a virtue. Yet, today, gratitude is often discounted as unsophisticated optimism or devalued as a polite social response. However, scientists who study gratitude characterize it as a complex, social emotion with distinctive qualities and an inherent social purpose.

Gratitude must be differentiated from seemingly similar thankful emotions. At one end of the spectrum, there is appreciation, which is the "recognition and enjoyment of the good qualities of a person or thing;" while, at the other end, one finds indebtedness, which makes the recipient feel compelled to "compensate the benefactor, not because recompense is a pleasure, but because obligation is a pain;" this can lead the recipient "to avoid and even resent the benefactor."[1]

Ultimately, four elements distinguish gratitude from other forms of thankful recognition and hint at its complexity:

· **The benefit was unexpected and unearned.** Gratitude is sparked when a benefit is provided that was not requested, expected or earned. By extension, the benefit is not part of a service one felt they had paid for but is something exceptional that likely required discretionary effort by the giver.

· **Receipt of the benefit moves the receiver.** Those experiencing gratitude don't just take the benefit received in stride. It touches them. It emotionally moves them. It has an essence of awe or wonder or humility that gives it meaning beyond simple recognition of the value of the benefit received.[1]

· **The intention behind the good deed matters.** To inspire gratitude, the benefit must be intentionally bestowed by the giver. Further, a recipient's perception of why a benefit was given drives the likelihood to feel gratitude. When a recipient

4

feels the action is rooted in genuine care and goodwill because the giver understood and cared about her, she is more inclined to both experience gratitude and to reciprocate the kindness.[2]

· **Gratitude is action-oriented.** Dr. Robert A. Emmons of the University of California, Davis, is one of the foremost thought leaders on the science of gratitude. He shares that gratitude is an action. It isn't just something to be felt but something to be expressed and acted upon. Further, Emmons says, expression is "an especially critical aspect of gratitude" that motivates us to recognize "either the person who has gifted us or more generally by passing on the goodness we have received to others. The expressions of gratitude go beyond a simple tit-for-tat reciprocity. Gratitude felt can even inspire great acts of charity and philanthropy."[3]

Embracing the many facets of gratitude leads to a working definition rooted in science and psychology:

Gratitude is sparked when someone freely and intentionally chooses to provide a worthwhile benefit to another person.[4] The benefit is unexpected, unsolicited and unearned by the recipient;[1] and the recipient intuits the giver helped out of a sense of genuine help and concern for her.[2] Receiving the benefit emotionally moves the recipient in a way that creates a sense of wonder, insight and humility[4] that inspires her to desire to reciprocate the goodwill to the giver or to others.

Simply, gratitude acknowledges a human connection by recognizing and joyfully returning unexpected and unearned expressions of kindness that were meaningful to the recipient.

A CONNECTION TO SOMETHING BIGGER

Gratitude doesn't just light up your face; it also lights up your brain. Neuroimaging of the brain lets scientists visualize how brain

THE PARTS OF GRATITUDE

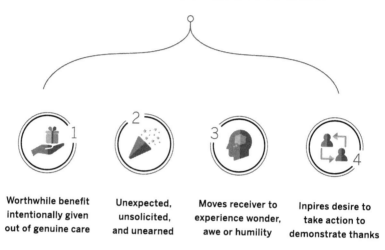

| Worthwhile benefit intentionally given out of genuine care | Unexpected, unsolicited, and unearned | Moves receiver to experience wonder, awe or humility | Inpires desire to take action to demonstrate thanks |

FIGURE 1.1

regions process information by making areas "light up" on a scan. When someone experiences gratitude, it not only activates the brain's pleasure and reward center but also affects areas associated with morality, connecting with others and taking their perspective.[4] So, gratitude doesn't just "feel good" but also compels the recipient to consider the rightness of connecting with others.

Thus, scientists characterize gratitude in action as a type of social glue that functions to strengthen relationships between people and to facilitate social bonding that safeguards well-being.[5, 6] When a grateful person demonstrates responsiveness to the giver's needs, it establishes a "reciprocally-altruistic" relationship that is said to help secure human survival by motivating people to attach to others inclined to help them.[7]

As gratitude pushes a grateful person to connect with those who have helped her, it also expands one's worldview beyond herself to motivate other-centeredness. The intrinsic motivation to focus on

6

others aligns with research that indicates people are hard-wired to seek connectivity and purpose and to contribute to something greater than themselves.[8] Making a positive impact in an area of personal significance allows people to achieve self-fulfillment and to realize their individual potential.[9]

There is an amazing, virtuous circle to other-centeredness. Those who experience and express gratitude create an unsought ripple effect of benefits in their own lives. Those who recognize, feel and express gratitude are rewarded with positive mental health benefits including increased happiness, motivation, optimism and reduced stress.[10, 11] Those with a grateful outlook also experience physical health benefits, including improved ability to heal. Dr. Robert A. Emmons shares:

"There is healing power in gratitude. We have the evidence. It's impressive and growing every day. Gratitude has achieved so much traction because of its healing ability. A host of new research studies are examining the effects of gratitude on health outcomes using state-of-the-art measures of biomarkers of health and aging. Clinical trials indicate the practice of gratitude can have dramatic and lasting effects in a person's life. It can lower blood pressure, improve immune function and facilitate more efficient sleep. Gratitude reduces lifetime risk for depression, anxiety and substance abuse disorders. It is a key resiliency factor in the prevention of suicide. In the latest findings, gratitude has been shown to be associated with higher levels of good cholesterol (HDL), lower levels of bad cholesterol (LDL), lower levels of both systolic and diastolic blood pressure (both at rest and in the face of stress), higher levels of heart rate variability (a marker of cardiac coherence), lower levels of creatinine (renal functioning) and lower levels of C-reactive protein (a marker of cardiac inflammation indicating heart disease). Grateful people engage in more exercise, have better dietary behaviors, are less likely to smoke and abuse alcohol and have higher rates of medication adherence. Gratitude is good medicine!"[12]

In short, scientific evidence clearly affirms gratitude not only feels good...and inspires us to do good...but is also good for us.

CONNECTING SYNERGISTIC VIRTUES

As gratitude both inspires other-centeredness and motivates meaningful connection with others, it seems natural philanthropy would become a logical outlet for expression. After all, philanthropy is also a humane and values-driven endeavor.

There is merit to elevating understanding within the health care organization that philanthropy springs from virtuous intent. The concept of philanthropy as a vibrant expression of love for mankind may be foreign to those accustomed not to see "philanthropy" but to see "fundraising." Since transactional "fundraising" often carries a negative connotation of arm twisting and imposition, it is understandable caregivers hesitate to engage with patients and families around something they feel is tainted. Therefore, it must be illuminated within

> "Gratitude flows from the recognition that who we are and what we have are gifts to be received and shared. Gratitude releases us from the bonds of obligation and prepares us to offer ourselves freely and fully."[13]
>
> Henri J. M. Nouwen,
> *A Spirituality of Fundraising*

the organization that the Greek "philanthrōpia" brings together "phil-" meaning "loving" and "anthropos" referring to "mankind" to reflect an intrinsically motivated benevolence toward one's fellow man. Expanding understanding about philanthropy as a joyful and meaningful expression through which a giver positively impacts the world provides a new context for meaningful conversation and restores philanthropy's beautiful legacy and intent to express altruistic care and concern.

"Gratitude-driven philanthropy would be a natural extension and continuation of the clinical experience," says Dr. Emmons. "It is important for us not to keep our thanks silent…Gratitude requires action. There is the action tendency of paying back the goodness that we have received. Gratitude will not strengthen relationships if it remains silent. We are grateful for the opportunity to give, because it reminds us that we too are dependent on the kindness of others in order to flourish."[12]

Ultimately, gratitude and philanthropy are a natural and marvelous combination with the potential to connect grateful goodwill with possibilities to create positive social impact. However, this alchemy of virtue does not happen in a vacuum. First, a fertile field must exist in which gratitude can grow.

CREATE A FERTILE FIELD FOR GRATITUDE

Dr. Robert Emmons says he is often asked how to inspire gratitude in others, and he replies, "we cannot give to others what we ourselves do not have." He continues, "Because gratitude is a virtue, it is more *caught* than *taught*. Gratitude must be modeled. The same holds for a clinical setting; gratitude must be modeled by the health care team."

Yet, it is obviously impossible to command clinicians or employees to *be grateful*. Doing so would be like insisting someone loves or forgives or trusts; experiencing emotion or embracing virtue is reliant upon the individual.

Unfortunately, gratitude in the workplace must often spring from barren soil. Employees feel vulnerable about expressing their own gratitude at work—with concerns ranging from fear of looking weak to feeling coworkers would take advantage of them to concern acknowledging the contributions of others toward their work could diminish their opportunities for advancement.[14, 15] Therefore, it is inherent upon health care leaders to proactively create a culture and environment conducive to individuals recognizing, receiving, sharing and celebrating gratitude.

Craig E. Deao is Senior Leader with Studer Group and author of *The E-Factor: How Engaged Patients, Clinicians, Leaders, and Employees Will Transform Healthcare*. Deao notes, "Leaders create the large environment and individual relationships conducive to commitment. Leadership role modeling is essential, since a leader's actions radiate onto her team. When leaders radiate positive energy, give credit to others and share their personal gratitude for work done well; it creates an environment to enable the team to do the right thing and to inspire discretionary effort when nobody else is watching."[16]

Positive modeling by organizational leadership accelerates acceptance and repetition of virtuous behaviors. Leaders demonstrating positive emotions enhance positive dynamics and emotional well-being in the workplace that, in turn, enhance employee relationships with others.[17] Further, research reiterates the importance of gratitude saying, "compassion begets gratitude" and "gratitude motivates improved relationships."[18] Further, leaders embracing "transcendent meaning, caring and giving behavior, gratitude, hope, empathy, love, and forgiveness" predict employee "commitment, satisfaction, motivation, positive emotions, effort, physical health and psychological health."[18] Expressing gratitude in the workplace also has a "spillover effect" that benefits workplace morale and cohesion by making individuals "more trusting with each other and more likely to help each other out."[15]

There is then a distinction between an organization where employees express gratitude to each other and an organization where gratitude is culturally embedded as an enduring and visible part of daily work life.[18,19] An organizational culture that authentically embraces gratitude recognizes the flow of gratitude throughout the organization. For example, conversations about gratitude in health care almost exclusively explore the patient's response to receiving care, yet patients aren't the only ones touched by gratitude: gratitude is multi-directional. The grateful organization not only sees gratitude from patients to caregivers and between members of the care team but also stirs self-awareness of a clinician's own sense of awe, wonder and humility for the privilege of being invited into the lives of patients and families during an experience marked by transformation, fear, hope and possibility.

Hospitalist Dr. Leif Hass of Sutter Health in California says physicians and clinicians can get so caught up in the logistics, time demands and pressure of administering care that they, "fail to see the real story is the patient's life, and thus they miss the gift that is the beauty of the lives before them. Crises from serious illness provoke existential struggles among patients and their families. Witnessing them firsthand is as rich an experience as life offers; being able to heal in this setting transforms a rich experience into a profound privilege and a gift." He says integrating a grateful outlook into practice can revitalize the work of health care professionals, since "recognizing the gift of someone placing their care in your hands makes one experience a surge of positive emotion and a desire to give back, which can motivate us to 'pay it forward' by helping someone else."[20]

An organizational culture where multiple avenues for gratitude are expressed, acknowledged, acted upon and celebrated amplifies virtuous emotion, positive energy and purpose-driven action.

INSPIRED SERVICE BEYOND ROLE

The health care organization culture must not only support caregivers in living gratefully but also inspire caregivers to tap into the purpose and meaning of their work as a motivation to provide exceptional patient experiences.

Returning to the clinical definition of gratitude, one must also consider gratitude is sparked by receipt of a benefit that was *unexpected and unearned*. While the point of care is separated from the point of payment in the care environment, most patients feel they provided compensation in exchange for medical care—whether it was money, insurance coverage or something as distant as paying taxes. However, providing compensation spurs an expectation to receive appropriate medical care from qualified caregivers. So, gratitude is less likely to be motivated by the clinical and technical work to arrive at a diagnosis and to facilitate treatment, since that work was "earned" by compensation and was consistent with what one would expect a caregiver to do in her role. Rather, gratitude comes from discretionary effort to deliver a better patient experience--often marked by attention to social and emotional needs, compassion, time, attention or comfort.

This is consistent with trends showing service excellence scores and measures of patient experience are strongly driven by the social and emotional experience rather than the performance or outcomes of clinical interventions. Of loyal customers who give scores of five out of five on surveys about their experience, it has been noted that something "unexpected and memorable" needed to occur.[21] So, what's memorable? Research on unsolicited positive feedback from patients found the main theme to be compassion.[22] This once again affirms excellent care is not solely a technical pursuit; it is always first and foremost about caring for people.

Propensity to feel gratitude is also influenced by the intention of the person providing the benefit. A recipient intuits whether a benefit was motivated by a giver's role, by a *cost-benefit evaluation* or by *positive feelings for the recipient*; and gratitude generally occurs only when a recipient feels the action was rooted in genuine care.[2] Further, experts in both behavioral economics and comparative ethics say perceptions of intention are relative to normative beliefs and expectations about what a typical, fair, individual "should" do in this type of situation.[23,24,25] Simply, if clinicians attend to the physical, social and emotional needs of patients simply out of role-driven obligation, patients will likely sense caregivers are "going through the motions" rather than acting upon an authentic sense of care for the patient's wellbeing. Kindling gratitude depends upon caregivers going above and beyond to instill empathy, caring and kindness into otherwise routine work and to enable unexpected and memorable care experiences.

...excellent care is not solely a technical pursuit; it is always first and foremost about caring for people.

Nurturing gratitude that may result in philanthropy begins with caregivers connecting with transcendent beliefs that intrinsically motivate them to use discretionary effort to improve the well-being of others. True compassion and caring can't be scripted, required or faked; they are motivated by values and commitments that allow a higher calling to care thrive.

NO INHERENT IMPOSITION

Despite an avalanche of data affirming the mental, physical and social benefits of gratitude, physicians and clinicians still share trepidation about proactively engaging with patients and family members around expressing gratitude through philanthropic giving to benefit the health care organization.

The nursing frontline has often been particularly reticent to engage in activities related to philanthropy. They often express concern facilitating engagement of those who could be able or inclined to give would create a two-tiered care system where those with financial wherewithal or organizational loyalty receive a higher standard of care. Many also express objections that connecting those who are grateful with the philanthropy office would violate patient privacy—despite the fact HIPAA privacy rules clearly allow philanthropy professionals to have a range of information about patients receiving care including treating physician name and area of clinical service. Others express discomfort stepping outside the clinical role into the realm of discussing a patient's values, beliefs and charitable intent crosses an unclear boundary. Others feel interacting with patients with a desire to direct gratitude toward philanthropy may be unethical or will negatively impact their relationship with the patient. Many simply feel unprepared.

Such concerns and hesitations make it essential to take the focus off of money. The clinical frontline does not need to identify those who have discretionary income or significant assets; they need to spot those who feel genuine gratitude for care received and those who have wonderful stories they might wish to share and tell. Dr. Emmons notes, "This is really, really, really important. It's not about the gift. It's not about philanthropy. It's about the connection. Gratitude is the relationship-strengthening emotion. It's a reminder of all those who have done things for us that we could never do for ourselves."[12] It's simple: focusing on the humane virtue and connection rather than focusing on money means many objections are no longer relevant.

Focusing on values and beliefs rather than money aligns effectively with existing separations between the point of payment, to include insurance status, and the point of care delivery in a clinical care environment. For example, physicians and nurses are not charged with asking people for their insurance card before delivering the highest standard of care. They are simply charged to "do the right thing" to provide the scope and intensity of care indicated by the patient's condition. Further, the philanthropy office has access to rafts of wealth screening tools and analytics to identify those with financial capacity and prospectively with affinity to give, so there is little need to ask clinicians to identify money. Instead, there is an opportunity to simply ask caregivers to identify those motivated or moved by gratitude or those with wonderful stories about their clinical, emotional or social care experience. If caregivers uncover those who are committed or grateful advocates, the burden of uncovering the presence or absence of financial capacity can be done behind the scenes by philanthropy professionals.

Focusing on nurturing and connecting gratitude means there is no inherent moral conflict or imposition upon patients by simply serving as conduits and connectors for those who are self-motivated and emotionally compelled to express their gratitude. Dr. Emmons reflects, "Cultivating patient gratitude is the way of optimizing health, better performance, wholeness and wellness. When you give, it is more than giving your time, resources or even 'capital;' fundamentally, it's about giving of your whole self. Gratitude is healing. The joy and happiness created by gratitude also leads to healing and healthier behavior. Therefore, it is imperative to facilitate increased opportunities for gratitude in the patient. In fact, I would go so far as to say that not giving opportunities for gratitude or not receiving gratefulness expressions well can be harmful to health." Further, "There is value in thinking of health care professionals as gratitude facilitators. I believe for maximal effectiveness, grateful patient programs must be part of a larger context for 'allowing' gratitude to flourish." There is no imposition or ethical burden in welcoming authentic connections around a meaningful human experience.

SPOTTING GRATITUDE IN ACTION

As consciousness of gratitude seeps into the organizational culture, caregivers can adopt a proactive approach to spot patient and family gratitude in action. Spotting gratitude is not always as simple or as straightforward as it sounds. Patients and family members may not say something as direct as, "I am so grateful for the quality of care / service I received!"

Instead, caregivers must be prepared for patients and family members to share gratitude in indirect ways. For example, a grateful patient or family member may say something like:

· My outcome exceeds my expectations.
· I'm really interested in <this aspect of clinical work /organization/ mission>.
· I've really been surprised by <positive aspect of care experience.>.
· I'd love to know more about <clinical work / caregiver / research /etc.>.
· What are the latest advances in <clinical service / clinical research>?
· You really made me feel confident and comfortable through this experience.
· So, what's it like to work here at <facility>?
· How is health care reform impacting your ability to do great work?

A valuable tool for uncovering gratitude comes from a leader in the service industry. At The Ritz-Carlton, everyone involved in the guest experience from the frontline to the back office is taught to look for the *unexpressed* needs of guests. They call the approach "Radar On and Antenna Up," and it guides all who come into contact with guests to be proactively alert. The premise is that just *responding* to articulated needs isn't enough to delight guests. So, "Radar On and Antenna Up" teaches everyone to look for subtle signals. In the health care environment, keeping our own radar and antennae attuned to how gratitude is verbally, physically or otherwise expressed is imperative to building a culture that agilely embraces gratitude. Raising individual and organizational consciousness of spotting gratitude is essential to supporting grateful engagement.

GRACIOUSLY ACCEPT GRATITUDE

Accepting gratitude is an appropriate part of each caregiver's role to provide holistic care. Yet, there is a tendency for caregivers to deflect thanks or to minimize the action that inspired it. Many deflect expressions of gratitude to exhibit humility. Others are embarrassed or flustered by praise or are unsure how to respond. However, awkwardness in acceptance often results in expressions of gratitude being met by pithy or rote responses that feel like a form of rejection to those expressing thanks; and this unintentional slight must be intentionally addressed.

Accepting gratitude graciously begins with avoiding inauthentic politeness and routine responses. Caregivers often admit they are "not sure what to say" and consequently default to the social norm of "you're welcome" in response to an expression of gratitude; however, this auto response is generally seen as hollow or dismissive by the expresser of thanks. Other common responses or deflections to avoid include:

- I didn't really do anything.
- Anyone would have done that.
- I can't accept credit for what happened.
- You don't need to thank me.
- It's all in a day's work.
- It's not a big deal.
- It's just what we do.
- Think nothing of it.
- No problem.

· No worries.
· I was just doing my job.
· Don't mention it.
· We got lucky.

No caregiver answered the calling to heal or to care in order to rebuff or diminish their patients. No one came to the mission of health care to only attend to the body and to ignore the emotional, social and spiritual aspects of care. So, with total care in mind, it's time to utilize more resonant and authentic expressions to acknowledge gratitude.

In responding meaningfully, it is still okay to use simple responses, as long as the expresser of thanks knows he was genuinely heard, seen and appreciated. For example, instead of responding with "you're welcome" consider responding with "thank you so much." That feels much less like, "you're right, I did do something worth thanking me for" and instead acknowledges a shared human connection. However, then consider what else might be authentically added to respond to that particular person in that particular situation to strengthen a simple thanks. For example:

· "Thank you. It has truly been a privilege to care for you."
· "Thank you. Your kind words really mean a lot to me."
· "Thank you. Your courage through all you faced has been inspiring."
· "Thank you. I have genuinely enjoyed getting to know you and your family."
· "Thank you. I'm glad you're well and able to return to the activities you enjoy."
· "Thank you. I'm glad to be part of something that was meaningful to you."
· "Thank you. Comments like yours are a real encouragement to our team."

As individuals become comfortable as gracious receivers of gratitude, they can explore other ways to resonantly accept gratitude. For example, one can often easily open the door to further feedback and conversation by asking a question that explores the source of gratitude in more depth. One can also use this opportunity to manage up others on the care team or clinical service by expressing why the expression of thanks would mean a lot to the team or aligns with efforts the team has worked hard to achieve.

Once caregivers master the art of receiving gratitude, it becomes easier to walk through the doorway to connect gratitude to giving. Once the expression of thanks has been appropriately and graciously acknowledged, the caregiver must bring her own intuition to the task to determine if the objective was simply to verbalize thanks or whether the expresser of thanks was receptive to or seeking to get more engaged. Sometimes, simply verbalizing thanks was the action. Therefore, sometimes caregivers need to decide whether they should "walk through" the door the patient has opened by expressing thanks to see if there is a desire for further connection or engagement. This can be done through advancing the conversation by seeking permission to expand the relationship, such as:

Weaving gratitude into the health care organization as both a touchstone and a compass can transform both the patient care experience and philanthropy.

> · "We really could use your help here. Would it be OK for me to put you in touch with someone from my team who could tell you more about our future plans?"
> · "There are a lot of ways to get more involved in our work. Would you like for me to introduce you to someone who could tell you about opportunities?"

· "Right now, we have some really exciting plans that might interest you. Would it be alright for me to include you in <upcoming meeting or event>?"

· "I really appreciate your interest. I have been working with a trusted partner from the philanthropy office. Would you like for me to connect you with <name>?

· "Your story is really inspiring. Would you be interested in sharing your story?"

When caregivers connect care to giving by introducing those who are grateful to philanthropy professionals who can articulate the current vision of the organization, it can be the catalyst to convert the grateful patient or family's intent to express gratitude into social impact. This not only allows the patient or family to achieve the good they have in mind but also provides closure for the care experience.

IN CONCLUSION:

As philanthropy professionals, there is an opportunity to simultaneously catalyze the potential of donor investment in the mission while remaining steadfast in adhering to the conscience and humanistic cultural values inherent in both health care and philanthropy.

Weaving gratitude into the health care organization as both a touchstone and a compass can transform both the patient care experience and philanthropy. Philanthropy is part of the healing process, and health care leaders need to begin viewing philanthropy as essential rather than as an add-on. Engaging physicians and clinicians to embrace, nurture and connect gratitude is not only patient-centered and beneficial to advancing philanthropy but also can provide them with personal meaning and benefit--just as philanthropy professionals see the invitation to make a charitable gift as a mutually-beneficial experience for both the donor and the organization. Philanthropy professionals can also support the engagement of physicians, clinicians and others by demonstrating personal integrity in all interactions to build a bedrock of earned trust.

Ultimately, infusing health care organizations with a spirit of virtuous gratitude and raising awareness of the transcendent beliefs, values and purpose that fuel a clinician's calling creates other-centeredness in both patients and caregivers that is human and humane. Philanthropy is part of the healing process, and health care leaders need to begin viewing philanthropy as a must have rather than an add-on.

Embracing gratitude and inspiring purpose-driven effort can also transform philanthropy.

Author's note:

Dr. Robert A. Emmons of the University of California, Davis, is one of the foremost thought leaders on the science of gratitude. I would be remiss not to note his truly gracious spirit and contributions here in both considering gratitude in a health care setting and in inspiring me to reflect the profound power of the virtue of gratitude.

References & Endnotes

1. Neel Burton, "The Psychology of Gratitude," Psychology Today (September 23, 2014): https://www.psychologytoday.com/blog/hide-and-seek/201409/the-psychology-gratitude.

2. Ames, D., F. Flynn, and E. Weber, "It's the Thought that Counts: On Perceiving How Helpers Decide to Lend a Hand," Personality and Social Psychology Bulletin 30 (2004): 461-474.

3. Robert A. Emmons, Gratitude Works (San Francisco: Jossey-Bass, 2013), 52.

4. Robert A. Emmons, The Little Book of Gratitude: Create a Life of Happiness and Wellbeing by Giving Thanks (London: Hachette, 2016).

5. McCullough, M.E., M.B. Kimeldorf, and A.D. Cohen, "An Adaptation for Altruism: The Social Causes, Social Effects, and Social Evolution of Gratitude," Current Directions in Psychological Science 17 (2008): 281-285.

6. Algoe, S., J. Haidt, and S. Gable, "Beyond Reciprocity: Gratitude and Relationships in Everyday Life," Emotion 8 (2008): 425-429, doi: 10.1037/1528-3542.8.3.425.

7. Algoe, S.B., "Find, Remind, and Bind: The Functions of Gratitude in Everyday Relationships," Social and Personality Psychology Compass 6(6) (2012): 455-469.

8. Susan Fowler, "What Maslow's Hierarchy Won't Tell You about Motivation," Harvard Business Review (November 26, 2014).

9. Paul Lawrence and Nitin Nohira, Driven: How Human Nature Shapes Our Choices (San Francisco: Jossey-Bass, 2002).

10. Amy Morrin, "7 Scientifically Proven Benefits of Gratitude that Will Motivate You to Give Thanks Year-Round," Forbes (November 23, 2014).

11. Dunn, E.W., et al, "In Praise of Gratitude," Harvard Mental Health Letter (November, 2011).

12. Dr. Robert A. Emmons to Betsy Chapin Taylor, Ponte Vedra Beach, FL, August 22, 2017.

13. Henri J. M. Nouwen, A Spiritualtiy of Fundraising (Nashville: Upper Room Books, 2010), 57.

14. Kira M. Newman, "How Gratitude Can Transform Your Workplace," Greater Good Magazine (September 6, 2017).

15. Jeremy Adam Smith, "Five Ways to Cultivate Gratitude at Work," Greater Good Magazine (May 16, 2013).

16. Craig E. Deao, interview by the author, Ponte Vedra Beach, FL, September 1, 2017.

17. Frederickson, Barbara L. and Thomas Joiner, "Positive Emotions Trigger Upward Spirals Toward Emotional Well-Being," Psychological Science 13:2 (March 2002): 172-175.

18. Cameron, Kim S., "Responsible Leadership as Virtuous Leadership," Journal of Business Ethics 98:1 (2011): 25-35.

19. Donaldson, S.I., M. Csikszentmihlyi, and J. Nakamura, et al, Applied Positive Psychology: Improving Everyday Life, Health Schools, Work, and Society (East Sussex: Routledge, 2011), 171-183.

20. Leif Hass, "Why Health Professionals Should Cultivate Gratitude," Greater Good Magazine (July 26, 2017).

21. Fred Reichheld, The Loyalty Effect: The Hidden Force Behind Growth, Profits, and Loyalty (USA: Harvard Business School Press, 1996).

22. Fred Lee, If Disney Ran Your Hospital: 9 ½ Things You Would Do Differently (Bozeman: Second River Healthcare Press, 2004).

23. Bicchieri, C., A Taste of Fairness. Philadelphia: University of Pennsylvania, 2005. Accessed September 13, 2017. http://www.dif.unige.it/epi/networks/05/bicchieri.pdf.

24. Christina Bicchieri, The Grammar of Society: The Nature and Dynamics of Social Norms (Cambridge: Cambridge University Press, 2006), 100-137.

25. Ma, Lawrence K., Richard J. Tunney, and Eamonn Ferguson, Gratefully Received: Gratefully Repaid: The Role of Perceived Fairness in Cooperative Interactions," PLOS One (December 8, 2014).

CHAPTER 2

Operationalizing Physician Engagement

Steven A. Rum

Grateful patient development (GPD) is, by far, the source of greatest potential revenue for hospitals and health care systems, offering the highest return on investment. Any philanthropy office in a health care setting, if it seeks to truly elevate gift revenue for the organization, should focus on establishing or strengthening its own GPD program. Yet, despite the centrality of GPD to health care development success and the many conference presentations, workshops, articles and webinars that focus on this topic, many philanthropy organizations are underprepared to advance this critical strategy.

The ability to educate, engage and, most importantly, change the behavior of physicians, organizational leaders and philanthropic gift advisors is the key to a successful GPD program. Engagement of physicians and other partners can only take place if the philanthropy office has succeeded in building a culture of philanthropy throughout the organization. After a brief discussion of the elements of culture creation, this chapter will address the core components of physician education and engagement: ethics, role definition, confidentiality and other legal issues, stewardship and an action plan.

CULTURE OF PHILANTHROPY

Regardless of a hospital's size, a GPD program will succeed only to the extent that it is part of a culture of philanthropy at the organization. Without a culture that values and actively encourages giving, the best strategic plans, presentations and personnel can have only limited impact.

Culture begins at the level of organizational leadership. Presidents and chief executive officers, deans and department chairs, lead physicians and faculty – all must believe in the importance of philanthropy to the organizational mission and must model a commitment of their time and resources to the development effort.

Without a culture that values and actively encourages giving, the best strategic plans, presentations and personnel can have only limited impact.

They must demonstrate philanthropy is "part of what we do for our patients, physicians, nurses and staff." Here, the phrase "for our patients" is critical.

Giving benefits the grateful patient/donor as well as the physician/organization. This vital fact is often overlooked, and failure to recognize donors' own interest in giving, and the fulfillment it can provide them, too often prevents GPD from being embraced by the organization. Leadership at all levels—medical, administrative, philanthropy and volunteer—must prioritize patients' experiences and understand their commitment and passion for change, which they hope to affect through philanthropy, is integral to their experience. Giving, itself, can be healing. Grateful patients are inspired by the care they've experienced and seek to give back. Our role is to facilitate a process in which they can add meaning, often accompanied by a sense of contribution which is both gratifying and healing to their lives.

The creation of a culture of philanthropy takes years, not months, to build. It is not created from any one event or team training exercise, but from daily—yes, daily—practices in which we champion the attributes of the grateful patient experience within the established internal system. The single biggest threat to a culture of philanthropy, and the most common reason for failure to adopt a true GPD program, is turnover by high-level philanthropy professionals. This turnover undermines the GPD culture, as it indicates a lack of credibility and sincerity on behalf of not only the particular philanthropy leader but also the profession of health care fund development. As philanthropy leaders succeed one another at an organization, they reinvent GPD programs, create new "strategic plans" and often bring in consultants in a repeated cycle of starting and stopping. Naturally, physicians and administrative leaders lose confidence, and their commitment to working with development diminishes. The culture of philanthropy erodes if it existed or cannot take root if not present.

Figure 2.1 depicts the centrality of culture to a successful GPD program. Truly, none of the components of a GPD program can thrive without a culture of philanthropy, without an endemic long-term commitment to encouraging philanthropy—large and small—at the organization. This culture cannot be assumed; it is explicitly taught, recognized and shared with audiences inside and outside the organization. Stakeholders must repeatedly receive the message through many channels that the benefaction of our patients, who have experienced superior care and who want to help us improve medical care for others, is integral to our mission and our greater impact. For many health care organizations, it is also key to survival in a competitive environment.

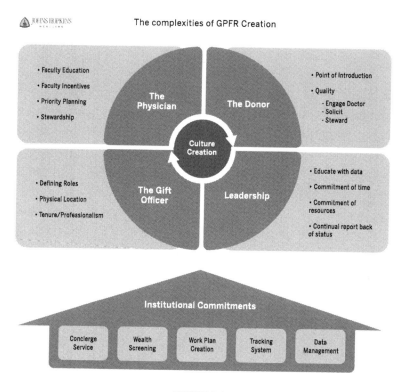

The complexities of GPFR Creation

- Faculty Education
- Faculty Incentives
- Priority Planning
- Stewardship

The Physician

The Donor

- Point of Introduction
- Quality
  - Engage Doctor
  - Solicit
  - Steward

Culture Creation

- Defining Roles
- Physical Location
- Tenure/Professionalism

The Gift Officer

Leadership

- Educate with data
- Commitment of time
- Commitment of resources
- Continual report back of status

Institutional Commitments

| Concierge Service | Wealth Screening | Work Plan Creation | Tracking System | Data Management |

FIGURE 2.1

It takes at least three years of ongoing—daily, weekly, monthly—cultivation and articulation to create a successful GPD program. The sections below describe key components of a high-quality, professionally defensible, physician education program in GPD.

PHYSICIAN EDUCATION

Nowhere in their medical education are physicians taught about philanthropy and the processes entailed in development. Educating physicians about GPD instead falls on philanthropy professionals and consultants, who promote myriad "best practices" through articles, workshops and programs. Their strategies can be didactic, experiential, group or individual, remote or in-person. These various strategies have been anecdotal "best practices" rather than evidence-based methods. Virtually all of the best practices taught throughout development for GPD rely on experience but have not been studied through empirical research.

What really works to engage physicians with a development team in actively identifying and enlisting patients with the potential and interest to give? One study, conducted at Johns Hopkins and published in the peer-reviewed journal *Academic Medicine* compared the outcomes of three methods of educating physicians about GPD: email, group lecture delivered by a physician with successful experience in development or one-on-one coaching by a philanthropy professional. The coaching intervention was based upon training models used in other fields, such as fitness, finance, management and leadership, where one-to-one support results in true behavioral change at a faster pace. The Hopkins study demonstrated one-on-one physician coaching was more effective than either group lecture or email education for generating physician referrals of grateful patients. Indeed, one-on-one coaching ultimately changed the behavior of physicians who participated in the study and resulted in new gifts and referrals.

The one-on-one coaching intervention covered five topics: (1) the ethics of GPD and its impact on the physician/patient relationship; (2) roles of the physician and the philanthropic gift advisor in the GPD process, at times also involving others in the organization; (3) legal issues, primarily focused on HIPAA and concerns about patient protection and organizational/physician liability; (4) time commitment and stewardship; and (5) an action plan.

1) Ethics of fund development

The single biggest challenge of engaging physicians in GPD is, typically, their fear that discussion of money will negatively impact their relationship with their patients. The Journal of Clinical Oncology drew attention to the lack of national guidelines with respect to the ethics and conduct of GPD. A philanthropy professional's ability to navigate this sensitive topic is vital to getting the physician to actively participate in the development process. Typical comments from the reluctant physician are: "I am not going to ask for money" or "I am just uncomfortable bringing up the topic of support for the hospital or any program" or "I don't want to be put in a situation where suddenly my patients are uncomfortable being around me in settings away from my clinic/office." At this moment, a philanthropy professional should begin to educate the physician on donor motivations, specifically citing not only national statistics about individual giving but also, and more importantly, specific examples of individual benefaction in the local community and how these gifts came about.

All giving is personal and results from a thoughtful, yet emotional, process; it serves both the giver and the receiver. Effective education about GPD will help the physician understand philanthropy is not extractive; it is an expression of an individual's positive personal experience, desire to give back or "do good" and passion for change. These gifts are the fruition reaped from the compassionate concern and care the patient received. Focused on the physician/patient bond, physicians often neglect to honor the sense of moral responsibility among philanthropists, at all levels of giving, for the greater good. The philanthropy professional can help a physician appreciate the patient's moral sensibility, and the generosity it inspires, by citing example after example of generous benefactors and their intentions. Qualms about ethics can often be resolved at this level, once the physician realizes giving is the patient's choice, and that the patient gains immeasurably through expressing generosity.

In educating physicians about the benefits of giving, philanthropy professionals should respect their legitimate concerns about timing.

> **Effective education about GPD will help the physician understand philanthropy is not extractive; it is an expression of an individual's positive personal experience, desire to give back or "do good" and passion for change.**

Physicians' fears that conversations about money may happen at inappropriate times, such as when the patient is physically or emotionally vulnerable, and that knowledge of a patient's wealth could drive disparities in treatment, are important. Philanthropy professionals must cite their experience in working with grateful patients, the measures they take to handle conversations with utmost ethical sensitivity and how partnerships evolve over time to a discussion about giving. Storytelling about real experiences of how patients came to be supporters-- and were excited, happy and gratified as a result of their giving-- are powerful. Physicians also need reassurance that patient care is never compromised by development activities, and that the quality and warmth of care for any given patient does not differ based on his or her wealth, though the level of stewardship provided to those who have been benefactors does differ.

Physicians' discomfort with GPD and their queasiness about ethics is often ameliorated when the philanthropic gift advisor clarifies the role each plays and defines the process of GPD.

2) Definition of roles

In a conversation with a physician, when defining who is responsible for which actions, the philanthropy professional should start with a simple question: "How comfortable are you with ...?", where the blank can be filled in by key role-defining elements of development including (a) identification of patients, (b) introduction of the philanthropy professional to the patient, (c) proposal development, (d) solicitation and (e) service and stewardship to the donor following the gift.

Let's begin with identification. Many organizations employ wealth screening services or some variation of "business intelligence" to gain insights about recent patients. Some even identify patients before their arrival for appointments, describe their net worth and estimate their capacities for giving. This level of qualification does not, however, mean an individual has a propensity to give; not all high-net-worth individuals qualify as prospects. Only after additional research, both formal and informal, should someone be considered a true prospect. Wealth-screened individuals are "suspects" until further investigation. Also important to note is, many times, wealth screening services miss names due to factors such as an inaccurate addresses; business intelligence is not 100% reliable.

Wealth screening can, however, be a good starting point for discussion of a patient with the physician. It can help the physician understand the concept of giving potential and can help him or her offer names of potential benefactors more frequently or more accurately in the future. Ultimately, the philanthropy professional should educate the physician that he or she, and not a wealth screening process, is the best source of business intelligence, and that one role of the philanthropic gift advisor is to train and support the physician in performing the screening role. These discussions go best when the conversation touches on a limited number of names at each one-on-one session; narrowing the focus makes the task seem manageable and allows for greater detail in discussing next steps with each patient. Too many names at any one sitting leads to a scatter-shot approach.

Physicians think of patients in terms of their health and disease, not their generosity; the physician's view of "who serves whom" is fundamentally unidirectional. The philanthropy professional must train the physician to think of patients as potential partners, as individuals who not only may have the capacity but also, most importantly, the desire to serve their physician in return through supporting his work or to serve the organization. This view is inherently bidirectional and requires considerable skill in listening.

Physicians need to learn to listen differently, if they are to pick up on cues related to capacity and interest in giving. They must first listen with their eyes. Instruct the physician not to be fooled by attire. Some of the wealthiest people in the community are some of the most conservatively dressed. Many people do not change their lifestyle just because they have "made it." Training a physician to be unbiased about a patient's appearance is difficult. It's easy to pick out the 10-karat ring or high-priced watch, but less straightforward to notice signs of hidden wealth. How are these people identified?

Physicians must learn to listen for cues that arise in natural conversation. The philanthropy professional can use role plays to train the physician to ask open-ended questions without being nosy. Guiding physicians through several practice conversations can give them a sense of confidence and add to their communication repertoire. For example, it is very natural to ask someone "what is it you do for a living?" It is a natural question that merely expresses interest in another. To continue this example, if the patient says, "I own a plumbing business," that is far different than saying, "I am a plumber." This type of information should be passed on to the philanthropic gift advisor. Since wealth screening only secures public information, there is little likelihood this gentleman's company, if 100% owned by him, will be picked up by wealth screening. Now, what if, upon further investigation by the philanthropy professional and team, they uncover the plumbing business owned by this gentleman has 125 employees and serves a substantial geographic region? The picture changes. Back-and-forth dialogue can take place casually and, through it, the physician and philanthropic gift advisor together can identify patients who may have both the capacity and the inclination to give.

Another innocuous question a physician can ask a patient is "Could you tell me about your family?" Many people appreciate this inquiry and will reply with insights that can give the physician clues about their lifestyle, priorities and even moral compass. As an example, adults who place a high value on family also tend to be committed to their community and to care about issues—such as health—that affect both.

The introduction of the philanthropic gift advisor is a critical next step, and a role that warrants explicit clarification for the physician. An unprepared physician can experience uneasiness as he tries to introduce a patient to a philanthropy professional.

Physicians stumble, for example, "I would like to introduce you to our, umm, external affairs person"—or "public relations" person or "community relations" representative. These awkward word choices are simply wrong. They misrepresent who the philanthropy professional is, and worse, they are likely to suggest the wrong expectations when the eventual meeting between the philanthropic gift advisor and prospect occurs. The relationship gets off on the wrong footing; the sense of transparency, collegiality and trust is sabotaged--sometimes irreparably.

The scripting of an introduction needs to be agreed upon and rehearsed. For example, the physician might state, in a comfortable manner, "Mr. and Mrs. Smith, I have enjoyed describing my project to manage diabetes in the community with you. With your permission, I would like to ask my colleague in development, Ms. Jones, to contact you to provide more information. Could she contact you by phone, letter or email--whichever is most comfortable to you? She knows my work well; and, in an introductory meeting, she could further describe it and answer any questions you may have." Or, "Mrs. and Mr. Smith, I would like to introduce you to our development person, Ms. Jones. She is responsible for the gifts given so graciously by individuals to benefit our hospital. Ms. Jones can explain to you in detail the challenges and opportunities for this community-based initiative." Present two or three possible opening lines to the physician in a one-on-one session to determine which one suits his style and, then, practice the script with him.

Many physicians simply won't make a personal introduction, and their desires should be respected. In this case, offer the second-best alternative—and name it as such--which is an introduction through a letter crafted by the philanthropic gift advisor but signed by the physician. The letter of introduction simply states, "I would like to introduce you to my philanthropic gift advisor, Ms. Jones. I have asked her to contact you in the near future to follow up on our conversation about the community-based program in diabetes management. Should you not want to be contacted by Ms. Jones, then please call my office, and I will ask her not to contact you." This letter is highly unlikely to ever lead to a recipient calling the physician's office to decline the conversation with the philanthropic gift advisor.

A letter is preferable to an email for a number of reasons. First, most people are inundated with emails on a daily basis. The recipient may ignore a new email, assuming it is an email "blast" rather than a personal overture from her physician. Secondly, and this is especially true of the older generation, people still like to receive postal mail, particularly personal letters. Stationary that is not standard 8.5" by 11" size stands out as different from bills, junk mail and solicitations. A personalized, non-standard letter shows the individual time has been taken to write to her specifically.

If the physician will not agree to a personalized letter, an email is the third preference, followed by a phone call from the philanthropic gift advisor without the benefit of physician introduction.

The script of the "warm call" made by the philanthropic gift advisor should also be shared with the physician, not only for reasons of trust and transparency but also to educate the physician about the philanthropic gift advisor's professionalism and style. Here, the philanthropic gift advisor has an opportunity to model effective, ethically sensitive, respectful and professional communication with the patient. An example is "Good afternoon, Mr. Smith. My name is Ms. Jones, and I represent the hospital and Dr. Kindness in the Department of Endocrinology." I work with Dr. Kindness as his philanthropic gift advisor. I understand you spoke with him about his community-based program for diabetes management. I am contacting you to ask if we might arrange a meeting between the two of us; or, if you'd like, Dr. Kindness can join us, so the three of us can discuss this program in further detail. I can assure you, the purpose of the meeting is not to discuss funding. It is simply to answer your questions and to describe what the challenges are and what the opportunities are for participation by you and other members in the community." By practicing this conversation out loud in front of the physician, he will gain a sense of how you conduct the phone call and can provide feedback that may help you tailor the call to the individual patient.

Proposal development follows a sincere expression of interest by, and often many conversations over several months with, the patient. The written word takes many different forms. Generally speaking, the higher the gift ask, the more specific the proposal. There is an art to engaging the physician in proposal development, as in other stages of gift cultivation from patient identification through stewardship. Physicians are busy people; many don't have the interest, time or talent to write an effective philanthropic proposal. Therefore, the process should start with the philanthropic gift advisor.

Taking a proactive approach in preparing the document helps to solidify the credibility of the development operation and keeps the process moving. A back-and-forth exchange in refining the proposal is necessary, but it can bog down the process. Explain to the physician that no document by itself is the basis for a decision to give, and excessive wordsmithing can delay matters for months with little value added. The proposal should provide a core reference point in support of the conversation with the donor or donor family.

Philanthropy professionals tend to place a lot of value on the aesthetics of a proposal, but pretty does not trump content. The proposal must accurately represent the need and the request, justify the amount of the ask and explain the uses of funds in sufficient detail to satisfy the donor. This is all part of education of the physician in GPD, as is the final presentation of the document. The preferred method, of course, is always delivery in person, with the philanthropic gift advisor and either the physician or an organizational leader present. Explain to the physician that a proposal just put in the mail and followed up with a phone call is the least desirable method; it has the least impact, fails to give the proper respect to the donor and suggests a mere "read over" of something sent. By contrast, "walking through" the proposal in-person with the donor demonstrates the seriousness of the ask and the importance the organization places on the relationship with the potential donor.

Timeline is a critical consideration in proposal development, and one which must be balanced against the physician's comfort level. The philanthropic gift advisor often must advocate for a timeline in the process, as the adage "time kills deals" applies to philanthropy. The emotions of the donor, and the sense of urgency of the organization or physician, must be taken into account when crafting the proposal and timeline.

Solicitation is the source of trepidation for many physicians, and a behind-the-scenes reason they hesitate to become involved in GPD. As a general rule, a physician should not ask for the gift for a number of reasons. Most do not want to make the ask; and, equally important, they are not good at it. If they receive a "no," it confirms their suspicion that we should not have been in this space; the relationship with development can be permanently damaged. Tell the physician, "You describe the program, and I will ask for the gift." If we are successful, the donor invariably turns to the physician with the affirmative answer, making her feel absolutely outstanding; if they say "no" or "not at this time," that statement is usually directed at the philanthropic gift advisor. Simply put, let the physician get the "yes" and the philanthropic gift advisor receive the "no." That slight deflection relieves the physician of any sense of rejection. Even if he is present in the meeting, the "no" is softer when it's directed to the philanthropic gift advisor.

When asking the questions "How comfortable are you with…?", the rare physician says, "I am absolutely comfortable in making the ask." In this situation, practice the script many times with the physician to observe and determine if further coaching is necessary. When initially discussing solicitation with the physician, preface the topic with "I don't ever want to put you in the uncomfortable position of making the ask. That's my job. I would prefer for you to describe the program or project. Then, when the time comes, I will make the ask." Additionally ask, "How comfortable are you being present when I make the ask?" Many times, the physician does not even want to be in the room when the philanthropic gift advisor is making the ask, and this should be clarified in advance.

When soliciting a grateful patient for a major gift, name the specific amount you are requesting after agreeing upon this amount with the physician, so there are no surprises. A philanthropic gift advisor should never hide behind a proposal that compels the prospective donor to find the request figure there. Be proud, even honored, to ask for a gift of a specific amount to support specific work at the organization you represent. Elicit their full attention. Make the ask when their eyes are looking at your eyes.

3) Legal issues

Why is it that, in one hospital, it is perfectly acceptable to discuss patient names with physicians and leadership while, in another hospital, this practice is considered inappropriate? Norms at organizations differ in large part because of differing interpretations by in-house legal counsel of the 2013 revised ruling of HIPAA (Health Insurance Portability and Accountability Act, 1996) called the Health Information Technology for Economic and Clinical Health ruling (HITECH). In the HITECH ruling, the federal government states, "In addition to demographic information, health insurance status, and dates of health care provided to the individual, (which currently is permitted under the Rule), this final rule also allows covered entities to use and disclose department of service information, treating physician information, and outcome information for fundraising purposes." The legislation clears the path for a philanthropy professional

Overcome legal gatekeeping by compiling an exhaustive list of hospitals that allow latitude in the disclosure of patient information and present this list to the chief medical officer and chief executive officer, asking for their support to change the organization's policy.

to have a conversation about engaging a grateful patient, yet some hospitals won't share patient names with philanthropy personnel. Why not?

After HITECH, a hospital's refusal to allow philanthropy professionals access to patient information is based on the lack of an organizational culture of philanthropy. Without a supportive culture, which includes and involves all stakeholders–from physicians to organizational leadership to patients—in the valuing of and the processes leading to giving, the acquisition of information about patients is viewed as unacceptable. Lawyers see organization "protection" as their role and step in to control the process.

Overcome legal gatekeeping by compiling an exhaustive list of hospitals that allow latitude in the disclosure of patient information and present this list to the chief medical officer and chief executive officer, asking for their support to change the organization's policy. Discuss the HITECH ruling with them. Ask them to explain why it isn't possible to share patient names between physicians and philanthropy professionals. At this time, there has never been a lawsuit, or even a threat of a lawsuit, from a hospital patient who sued because of a HIPAA violation on the part of a philanthropy professional.

4) Time commitment and stewardship

Often physicians are unclear about the development process after their patients make a gift and their role in these subsequent activities. Their question is, "What am I expected to do, now that they are benefactors?" In response, ask them, "What are you comfortable in doing?" The range is wide: Some physicians give donors their cell phone and home phone numbers with a message to "call me anytime should you have a health issue," while others don't want to feel like they are "owned" by the donor. (These fears are warranted. There have been some cases of real abuses by donors.) Generally speaking, instruct the physician that the more time you devote to relationship-building and maintenance with the donor, the greater the likelihood that he will come forth with further philanthropic support.

Relationship-building, outside of clinical visits, depends upon the physician's comfort level. There is a fine line between the clinic- or hospital-based physician/patient relationship and a friendship between the patient-now-donor and the physician – a rapport that continues outside the clinical setting. Only the physician can determine whether or not, and when, this line is crossed. Some physicians are comfortable, even enjoy, attending parties hosted by donors in their homes or clubs. Some feel uncomfortable. This should be discussed between the philanthropy professional and physician, touching on the potential pitfalls of such a friendship. For example, sometimes the relationship between a donor and a physician be-comes so strong outside the clinic that it becomes impossible to ask for a second gift, years later; the physician fears asking for a second gift will alter, erode or even terminate their friendship.

The difficult topic of "service" should be covered on a case-by-case basis with the physician prior to the ask. Some donors will require a lot of "service," while others won't require any. One-on-one coaching of the physician should clarify this and ensure the physician un-derstands the possibilities. Analogies help. For example, someone flying first class pays more and, in exchange, waits in shorter lines, gets a better seat and receives better food. But the pilot flies the plane equally well for every passenger, regardless of the amenities provided to some. Similarly, if a patient makes a significant gift to the physician and organization, they should not have to sit for long in the waiting room before their next appointment. It is reasonable to offer them a "concierge" experience, rather than asking them to work through the general appointment line. These sorts of service provided back to the donor complete the circle of giving and often lead to further giving.

Stewardship, and the continual engagement of the physician with the donor/grateful patient, is critical if the donor relationship is to grow. Stewardship is not synonymous with service. Because the first gift is the hardest to secure, and the first-time donor is the easiest donor to lose, stewardship begins immediately upon the donor's expression of gift commitment and often in anticipation of that commitment. A comprehensive one-year plan covering how the donor and family will be updated on the results of their generosity provides a roadmap for growing the relationship; the plan should be informative to relevant individuals including the philanthropic gift advisor, physician and organizational leadership.

Stewardship is a concept that must be taught to physicians. It expresses respect for the patient and family beyond just their wealth and philanthropic support. It affirms the value with which the organization and the physician hold them, and it is rooted in a culture of generosity, service and gratitude.

5) Action plan

In the philanthropy offices of most health care organizations, philanthropy professionals plan and document "moves" with respect to prospects. Similar to "moves management™" for donors, the concept of "moves" should be applied to physician engagement. In coaching the physician, the philanthropic gift advisor should take a series of steps to train the physician in GPD and successively build her skill in this competency area. This is an "action plan," which outlines the GPD process and its timing.

A first step in developing an action plan is to clearly state your intention to the physician with a statement such as: "My job is to identify what you are comfortable and uncomfortable with doing throughout these relationships, to identify and draw upon your strengths and to protect you from those elements of GPD which you do not feel prepared or willing to do. Together, based on your feelings and capacity, we will define your role and activities. I will take care of the rest." A successful action plan that covers the above categories in a thorough and honest discussion results in both the philanthropic gift advisor and the physician knowing their defined roles, achieves active discussion between them about identification of potential grateful patients and leads to timely introduction of these prospects to the philanthropy professional.

A proactive philanthropic gift advisor has a game plan at each step of the way, reports back to the physician on actions completed and describes next steps. This preparedness goes a long way toward establishing credibility with a physician which, in turn, supports the sort of development/physician partnership that moves the GPD process forward toward the ultimate goal—a significant gift made by a grateful patient to the physician and/or the hospital. For a philanthropy professional, there's no greater feeling. In the end, it is a sense of fulfillment shared by all, for it is not the money but its impact, along with the generosity and gratitude underlying it, that lend true meaning to the gift.

References

1. Rum, S. and S.M. Wright. "A Randomized Trial to Evaluate Methodologies for Engaging Physicians in Grateful Patient Fundraising." Academic Medicine 2012;87(1): 55-59.

2. Walter, J.K., K.A. Griffith, and R. Jagsi. "Oncologists' Experiences and Attitudes about their Role in Philanthropy and Soliciting Donations from Grateful Patients." Journal of Clinical Oncology 2015;33(32): 3,796-3,801.

3. Rum, S.A., J.L. Wheeler, and S.M. Wright. "Instituting and Teaching Ethical Standards for Grateful Patient Fundraising." Journal of Clinical Oncology 2016;34(12): 1,423-1,424.

CHAPTER 3

Enhancing Major Gift Performance by Blending Art & Science

Amy Grenzebach Day

The Chicago Cubs, known far and wide as the Lovable Losers, had not won a World Series in 108 years—the longest losing streak ever in professional sports. "Maybe next year!" was always the mantra. But on November 2, 2016, a miracle occurred ... except it wasn't.[1]

There is much leaders can learn about advancing philanthropy from the outcome of the 2016 World Series, accomplished through work that started long before.

At a recent Association for Healthcare Philanthropy (AHP) presentation, a room full of chief philanthropy officers was asked how many thought they could achieve breakthrough performance through better application of the art of development. Just a few hands were raised. When asked who thought they would achieve high performance through science, just about every hand went up.

Despite a growing interest in analytics and process improvement in development (though still lagging behind health care in general and society at large), so far only a small number of philanthropy organizations are applying the kind of science to fund development that will produce results anywhere near what brought the Cubs The Commissioner's Trophy.

Why not?

Inertia? Lack of know-how? Always settling for "maybe next year?"

To be fair, no. The answer requires recognizing a systemic obstacle many chief philanthropy officers have faced—and struggled with. And it's really three problems philanthropy professionals have in common with many baseball teams:

1. The "game" has long-standing traditions and is steeped in conventional wisdom;

2. There is a "star system" and little front-line teamwork; and

3. The "owners"- while quite successful in their own endeavors - have a cursory understanding of what the professionals do and how to do it better.

Before the "professionalization" of the fund development field, most efforts were simply based on individuals and their relationships with each other. For many years, development was on the shoulders of solo gift advisors who were either like cowboys in the Wild West--lonely, tough and independent--or those with star-like qualities with the ability to build strong relationships and secure gifts through the power of their personality. Fund development was all about personality and relationships. The most successful fundraisers had perfected this as an art.

As health care organizations increasingly feel financial pressure, philanthropy is beginning to be recognized as more than the "nice to have." Now, the challenge is to enable philanthropy to reach its full potential as a strategic service line, capable of producing the highest return on investment of any function in the health care organization. While hospital operating margins remain in the red or in the low single digits and borrowing involves significant costs, philanthropy has the potential to generate capital at a rate of return on investment of 75% or greater.

To achieve such high levels of return, chief philanthropy officers must focus their programs on major gifts. The 2015 AHP Report on Giving shows the highest performers in health care philanthropy derive 80-90% of their revenue from major gifts.[2] But, even with a clear body of evidence that major gifts are the engine to propel health care philanthropy to higher performance and greater impact on our organizations, shifting to a major gifts focus continues to be a significant challenge for chief philanthropy officers.

WHY? TRADITIONAL THINKING DICTATES OTHERWISE.

The theory behind the donor pyramid remains unproven, and the concept is increasingly irrelevant. However, conventional wisdom still calling for a well-rounded program drives staffing and resource allocation decisions. Competing demands for traditional, high-visibility activities such as legacy events, employee giving campaigns and annual direct mail programs distract from a focus on major gifts.

Finding and keeping competent philanthropic gift advisors is a significant challenge. With the annual tenure of a "major gifts officer" in the field abysmally low, one needs to only glance at the job postings to see demand far exceeds supply. Tradition dictates philanthropic gift advisors work alone, each with his or her own portfolio, each in his or her own unique way with the belief that the typical major gift takes 18 months or more to come to fruition. That is interesting considering philanthropic gift advisor turnover is rampant, and the average tenure is not much more than 18 months.[3] How can strong relationships be maintained and performance dramatically improved with such high turnover?

Boards ingrained in governance result in staff structures weighted toward administration, while board avoidance of involvement in major gift development denies front-line professionals the help they need in making connections. And expectations that chief philanthropy officers serve in a variety of internal leadership positions and that gift advisors also handle event responsibilities drain time away from major gift development.

But, worst of all, is the low level of expectation—and, consequently, investment—with which hospital leadership regards development.

Some board members understand the potential power of philanthropy to transform organizations. Too rare is the health care executive with a vision for philanthropy. Most are content with relatively mediocre performance from their philanthropy shops. A recent, in-depth study involving CEO interviews found almost every CEO had hopes and expectations of increased philanthropy in support of their organizations, but almost none could articulate a strategy beyond "hope" for better philanthropy results. However, if hope is our strategy, we're not well positioned for increased performance.[4]

Just like the Cubs in 2016, we need to break the "maybe next year" cycle of "hope without strategy." And, also like the Cubs, it is going to take a focus on both the art and science of development. The Cubs turnaround began long before results were seen on the field by employing the latest in science and analytics. They hired front office leadership with experience in "Moneyball" statistics, drafted the right players out of college and built a strong organization.[5]

INVEST IN SCIENCE

What we typically think of as the science of fundraising—analytics, prospect research, new technologies—is critical. Successful health care philanthropy organizations focused on major gifts must have the analytical tools, research capabilities and advanced constituent management systems. Prospect research, donor data analysis, patient screening and wealth ratings provide frequent opportunities to enter the highest potential prospects into the development process.

While these important tools are the focus of fund development's current "scientific" investments, there are two investments that will optimize performance in major gifts:

- · a disciplined process for moving prospective donors to a gift commitment and
- · a structured and process-based development services function.

Implement a Phase-Gate Process

A clearly defined, phase-gate process—such as the core process[6] —with the right technology support ensures philanthropic gift advisors focus on the highest potential prospects with the right cultivation activities for that individual. A process and an accompanying suite of reports also provide clear metrics and measures for the individual gift advisor and a management tool for the chief philanthropy officer.

Phase-gates are a business process model that originated in the for-profit world of innovation and product development and are relatively new to fund development. In major and principal gift development, phase-gates are used to clearly define when a prospective donor "moves" between stages and are more well-defined than a traditional Moves Management™ process. Simply defined, a phase-gate is the point (or gate) at which a decision is made to move the work to the next stage or decision point—or not.

The decision to move a prospect to the next stage is a critical one in major gift development. It is an outward statement about the commitment to continue to invest gift advisor time...

The decision to move a prospect to the next stage is a critical one in major gift development. It is an outward statement about the commitment to continue to invest gift advisor time (in increasing amounts as the process advances) on this prospect. That decision depends on whether certain criteria are met. For example, to "move" a donor into a portfolio, certain questions must be answered in a face-to-face meeting by a front-line philanthropic gift advisor to ensure there is proper capacity, interest and inclination to warrant moving forward. Questions that must be answered to proceed can include, "What are your top three charities of choice?" The process helps prepare the right information, with the right level of detail, at each gate to support the best decision possible. It empowers the team by providing a road map with clear decisions, priorities and deliverables at each gate. This also allows for accurate information related to the average time prospective donors remain in a particular stage or average time it takes from meeting a donor face-to-face to closing a gift, etc.

However, applying a rigorous process to relationship builders is not easy. Expect feedback that an experienced gift advisor's professional judgement is always superior to process, or that this is "killing the soul of development" and "interfering with the relationship" by dictating what step should come next. Yet, common impediments to performance are clear and result in wasted time and lackluster results:

· conventional moves management that does not move the donor along a charted path

· gift advisor time spent building relationships with donors who do not have the capacity or inclination to make a major gift

· human tendency to focus on the prospects with whom one is most comfortable, rather than those with the most potential

Leverage Development Services

Effectively employing a phase-gate process also requires an investment in a strong and robust "development services" function. The development services team is comprised of professionals oriented toward process who see the value in their work of both driving the prospect pipeline and ensuring the process remains focused and efficient. They are not administrative assistants but are professionals who understand the process of development—often better than the gift advisors. They drive metrics and are as critical to closing the gift as are the gift advisors themselves.

The development services function is critical to ensuring front-line philanthropic gift advisors have the prospective donors and resources they need to be out meeting face-to-face with donors, rather than being behind a desk writing proposals or typing contact reports. Development services professionals partner with gift advisors as they work through the process – ensuring a focus on the right prospects at the right time and contributing to their breakthrough success. It can be a challenge for a development services officer to point out to a gift advisor that the data shows a certain prospective donor will never make a major gift – but the success of the team requires it. At the same time, development services must remove all distractions from the field – delivering high quality and high reliability in work product – so gift advisors are open to do what they do best in building relationships.

INVEST IN ART

While the science—a robust prospect pipeline, a rigorous process and development services—is essential, it alone will not close more gifts. Major gift development is, and will always remain, an endeavor based in relationships. We must invest in philanthropic gift advisors who are relationship builders. Some of these qualities can be articulated through advancements in research in emotional intelligence and psychology. Daniel Goleman's five elements of emotional intelligence—self-awareness, self-regulation, internal motivation, empathy and social skills—provide a blueprint for the qualities that make a successful gift advisor. [7]

There are also intangibles to look for in philanthropic gift advisors. Prior development experience is not necessarily required. The best candidates are individuals who are curious about other people, have a sense of humor, are great storytellers, relate well with a wide variety of people, are confident and have energy or "sparkle." Most importantly, they need to have a sense of fearlessness. They cannot be afraid of "no."

Once these individuals are on the team, give them both the freedom to drive relationships based on their experience, instincts and ability to know what is best for the donor—as well as the process and metrics necessary to achieve an overall high level of performance. There are two investments that will increase gift officer performance: smaller portfolios and frequent coaching.

Utilize Smaller Portfolios

One concrete way to increase both the freedom provided to gift advisors to work their prospective donors and overall productivity is to reduce an individual's portfolio size. This seems counterintuitive and goes against current industry practice. However, an active portfolio size of 120 prospective donors does not lead to more productive gift advisors. In fact, it is just the opposite. Often, gift advisors are compelled to make contact with prospective donors assigned to a portfolio who do not have the inclination or capacity to give in the next 12 months, and those prospective donors routinely sit in a portfolio untouched. Take any portfolio of 120 and see if those donors with the most activity align with those with the greatest capacity. It is human nature to go where it is easiest: those who will take meetings easily or who are not as challenging. With gift advisors intentionally focused on a smaller number of prospective donors, it can create an environment of abundance through high volume input and reap much tighter cycle times from first meeting to close of the major gift. Of prospects in large portfolios, the reality is often only 20 are truly active in the sense that purposeful conversations are underway toward a gift.

Allowing gift advisors to focus on their 20 top active prospects provides them the opportunity to focus their work and interactions on closing the gift, rather than trying to maintain regular contact with so many individuals.

Allowing gift advisors to focus on their 20 top active prospects provides them the opportunity to focus their work and interactions on closing the gift, rather than trying to maintain regular contact with so many different individuals. However, reducing active portfolio size cannot be done in isolation. First, a phase-gate process is essential to ensuring the 20 prospects in the portfolio are the right prospects. As previously discussed, the phase-gate process provides regular opportunities through the development process to allow the philanthropic gift advisor and chief philanthropy officer to discuss, evaluate and measure whether a prospective donor is truly moving toward a major gift. Honest evaluation conversations about each prospective donor will ensure they have the capacity and inclination to provide a gift and that their philanthropic interests currently align with institutional priorities and needs.

In addition to the phase-gate process, a prospect management system with an evergreen list of prospective donors is critical to ensure there is a list of individuals to move into a gift advisor's top 20 active portfolio. Typically, this system involves a combination of prospect research, patient screening and board and physician referrals which results in 100 or more potential, prospective donors per gift advisor that is constantly being updated and adjusted—a critical function of development services. The end product is a focused portfolio of 20 active prospects for each gift officer and an evergreen list of prospective donors to add either when a gift closes or a determination is made through a phase-gate discussion to move the prospective donor out of the major gift process.

Develop a Culture of Coaching

Artists develop their skills through critiques by masters and other artists. They never assume they have arrived. And, while much of their success is due to innate talent, they improve through structured opportunities for critique (such as the salons of years past). Baseball players who are born with natural talent also invest significant time practicing with coaches and reviewing video to analyze their pitching, swinging or fielding to improve their skills.

Like artists and baseball players, coaching is critical to successful philanthropic gift advisors. Often, training of gift advisors is relegated to industry conferences or external consultants. While these can be valuable professional development tools, it creates diverse training methodologies and inconsistent processes within an organization. Coaching by the chief philanthropy officer and other senior professionals is critical to success and creates an environment with a high quality of work and increased employee satisfaction. Historically, the field's approach has been to hire gift advisors, assign them a portfolio and set them free to use their relationship skills as they see fit. While much of their success is based on existing skills, coaching will enhance a gift officer's qualities and build on their strengths. Building a culture of coaching allows gifts advisors to strategize with one another, formally and informally, while also providing continued development opportunities.

While building a culture of coaching requires building trust among the gift advisor team, there are four areas that can be developed to provide structure.

First, provide training on the development process the team is utilizing. Everyone involved in the major gift process, not only gift advisors, must understand what is expected to occur at each stage of the process. This training also includes suggested scripts, key questions and other messages that should be consistent in all donor interactions. These training sessions provide the background and common language for the other coaching activities.

Second, coaching on style, body language and other interpersonal cues is critical. A theoretical understanding of the development process and memorized scripts of meetings does not make for a good gift advisor. Perfecting the art of relationship building requires an examination of how one interacts with others and demands each gift officer develop his own language unique to his style. Role playing with the gift advisor and development services team provides the opportunity for practice, particularly for difficult or unexpected conversations. Video review of role playing is much more accessible now with smart phone technology. While often uncomfortable for gift advisors, review and critique of video playback provides heightened self-awareness and excellent coaching opportunities. These sessions should not be a one time or annual endeavor but should be scheduled regularly to allow for continual improvement and peer-to-peer coaching.

Third, the phase-gate process requires a weekly session to review phase-gate moves in the prior weeks. These meetings should be focused on those prospects who have accomplished the goals of their current stage and whom the gift advisor would like to advance to the next stage in the process. While these discussions first focus on the technical question of whether the stage objectives have been met, they should be coaching conversations with the philanthropic gift advisor. This is the opportunity to discuss how the relationship with the prospect is developing, strategies for the next stage and assistance needed in moving the relationship forward. If the gift advisor is recommending exiting the prospect from the major gift process, this also provides the opportunity to discuss the reasons and lessons learned for the future.

Finally, to build a culture of coaching, there must be openness to and desire for continued strategy sessions. These sessions may be formally planned (outside of the weekly phase-gate review sessions) with key players to complete a formal strategy document. They may also be informal, short, "water cooler" conversations amongst team members or with the chief philanthropy officer. There will also be daily discussion between gift advisors and development services professionals familiar with the process and with strategies of multiple gift officers. These strategy conversations are often the most important and impactful for gift advisors.

INVEST IN TEAMWORK

It would be self-defeating to invest in relationship builders and not provide them the freedom to do what they do best. A philanthropy organization's greatest resource is human capital, and it is critical to focus those resources on the highest value activity to achieve high performance. However, the lesson of Michael Lewis' bestselling book *Moneyball* was that star players by themselves don't create sustainably high performing teams.[8]

After the Cubs won the World Series, team ownership gave World Series rings to every member of the organization. Not just players and coaches--but everyone from scouts to analysts to accountants to security guards. Their celebratory parade and rally included the entire team, as well. They knew their breakthrough success was not just the result of the players on the field but of a team effort over several years. And, while the media focused on the players and manager, leadership focused on the entire team – knowing this success and future success would continue to be dependent on all involved. The same is true for the major gifts focused development team.

This partnership and teamwork requires mutual respect and a fondness for one another on the team. It's often said, "if you love what you do, it's not work." Now, take that one step further: if you love who you do it with, you just might bound out of bed every morning eager to join colleagues working toward collective goals. For philanthropic gift advisors, it is a pleasure to match those who have the ability and inclination to make a difference with audacious opportunities that light up their eyes and ultimately make a difference in our communities. Isn't that why people chose this profession? And, development services officers deserve equal credit for their equally important role in achieving the goals.

Orchestrating this magic is the job of the chief philanthropy officer, the general manager of the team. This involves demonstrating confidence in the team. When Joe Maddon, manager of the Chicago Cubs, was asked "Is it possible the Cubs can win the World Series?" he replied, "Of course, of course it is."[9] It is also important to create a culture of teamwork. As Theo Epstein, president of baseball operations of the Chicago Cubs put it, they asked players "to be themselves, to show their personalities, to have fun, to be daring, to be bold."[1] Those who have worked in a true high-functioning team know how joyful and how successful it can be. Treating philanthropic gift advisors well and beyond the metrics of number of solicitations made or dollars raised will engender both loyalty and longer tenures. Investing in talent reaps significant returns and creates teammates who never want to be traded.

Once the Cubs had pieces in place based on science, they shifted their focus to the art, and the fun, of baseball. They hired a manager who related well to players and focused on teamwork rather than individual all-stars. They knew keeping their players loose and away from the pressures of breaking a century long curse was essential. And, they built a first-class organization around the players of coaches, scouts, marketers and support personnel who let the players focus on the game. It was this blend of art and science and a focus on teamwork that led to the Cubs breakthrough.

BLEND NOT BALANCE

Has philanthropy gone too far in embracing the cliché of "balancing" the art and science of development? Many philanthropy professionals started out as gift advisors and were taught it is important to balance the art and science of development. However, "balance" implies this is a half and half proposition or suggests it is a 50/50 equation. Balance conjures up the image of a scale, always seeking equilibrium and dangerously close to tipping at any moment. Without a donor-centric process, the scale tips too far toward science, the connection becomes impersonal and philanthropy professionals lose that important emotional connection with donors. With too much focus on measures involving money, the pressure leads to transactional activity. Without metrics and process, interactions become less purposeful. Like a scale, without equal weights, the balance would become unstable and come crashing down. It's time to confront whether it is not "balancing" but rather "blending" to bring together and integrate qualities within a culture of teamwork that wins the World Series.

It is essential for the chief philanthropy officer to find the right blend of art and science to foster a focus on major gifts and to build the best team. For the Cubs, it was critical to first focus on the science, utilizing statistics to acquire players who also had character and valued teamwork. At the same time, they built a supportive organization and created a culture that eventually led those players to play championship baseball. Ultimately, that is the task: blend art and science to have the right team of philanthropic gift advisors with the best support possible and a culture of teamwork that allows them to thrive.

With advancements in technology, science will continue to improve performance and to provide solutions to challenges. We are increasingly employing analytics, new research tools and performance improvement methodologies, such as Lean Six Sigma, to advance our work. And this is understandable as our health care organizations move in this direction and as science has shown process-based, metric-driven organizations develop more capacity and deliver better results.

However, organizations may have the best data from patient screening and analytics, a robust prospect pipeline and evidence-based case materials and still not achieve success if there is not a culture of team work to let players play. So, how do we achieve breakthrough performance? We must invest in a blend of both science and art, and, equally important, invest in a culture of teamwork.

References & Endnotes

1. Epstein, Theo, "Yale University Class Day Remarks." Speech, New Haven, CT, May 21, 2017. Yale Website. yale.edu.

2. Association for Healthcare Philanthropy. "Report on Giving FY2015." ahp.org.

3. Association for Healthcare Philanthropy. "AHP 2016 Salary Report U.S." ahp.org.

4. Reed, Steven, "Hope Is Not a Strategy," Healthcare Philanthropy journal 41:2 (2012): 10-15.

5. Michael Lewis, Moneyball: The Art of Winning an Unfair Game (New York: W.W. Norton, 2004).

6. A phase-gate process first developed by consultant Steven Reed in 2003 to facilitate a $100 million campaign for Florida Hospital, Orlando. The role of the development services officer is integral to the process.

7. Daniel Goleman, Emotional Intelligence: Why it Can Matter More than IQ (New York: Bantam Books, 1995).

8. However, they also knew that other teams were also employing these tactics without similar results. They may have had the best players with the most potential according to statistics, yet their performance never matched their promise.

9. Jesse Rogers, "Joe Maddon: Cubs Continue to Play Better; Could Get to Playoffs, Advance," ESPN (August 25, 2015): espn.com.

CHAPTER 4

Using Metrics to Drive Top Performance

David S. Collis

Whether you raise \$1,000,000 or \$100 million, there are consistent metrics successful and sustainable philanthropy programs have in common. Tracking and improving performance in these areas drives excellence in both small and large programs. While fund development is a complex endeavor, setting specific, metric-driven activity and financial goals provides critical focus and reduces distractions.

SIMPLE AND FOCUSED

Philanthropic gift advisors have many competing demands for their time and attention. However, advancing the organization's mission through philanthropic investment in top initiatives should always be the top priority. Therefore, meeting with potential donors to share the organization's exciting vision for the future is critical to inspiring philanthropic gifts. So, what is the philanthropy team really focused on?

It has been said that what gets measured gets done. If the philanthropy organization is not tracking its most important activities—to include visits, solicitations and total dollars raised—you are already off-target. That's why it is important to select clearly defined and actionable metrics to focus work and to measure progress.

High performing organizations monitor and measure actionable indicators that are relevant to daily work and with a focus on visit, solicitation and financial metrics. In defining goals, keep them simple, and put them in writing. Do not make goals more complex than needed. Simple, actionable plans are easier to track and measure. A quicker feedback loop will help leaders make adjustments on-going. Keep plans specific and measurable with clear outcomes expected as a result of actions. This is key to ensuring success. Take the big picture vision and boil it down, so it is simple enough for everyone to understand and discuss.

Without professionally-driven development activity, analyzing financial metrics is putting the cart before the horse. Visit and solicitation activity are "LEADING" metrics/indicators of financial performance. Financial performance measures are actually "LAGGING" indicators. Without focus on the leading indicators of performance activity metrics, the organization cannot hope to drive high quality financial performance. Leaders cannot hope to steer a foundation to greater financial performance if the organization has not first mastered the true cause of financial success—a high performing philanthropy team focused on mission with specific visit and solicit metrics driven by a core process.

HARNESS THE POWER OF DATA

No matter the size of the philanthropy program, data can be the organization's strongest ally and most valuable asset. It can show if programs are headed in the right direction and where to make changes for greater success. Using data the right way also increases credibility with the C-suite, makes a compelling case to donors and sets clear expectations and goals for staff.

Today's philanthropy leaders use benchmarking to inform decisions, set goals, monitor progress and measure outcomes. For example, benchmarking is used to:

• Demonstrate value.
• Drive program refinement to maximize their impact.
• Track gift officer activity metrics such as number of contacts and number of solicitations on a weekly basis to help the foundation identify and address barriers to a gift officer's work in a timely manner.
• Measure the organization against similar systems on a number of metrics such as yearly contributions, number of FTEs and yearly contributions per FTE to gain insight into growing or stagnant revenue and to make the case for hiring more FTEs.

The Association for Healthcare Philanthropy's Performance Benchmarking Service provides a simple way for leaders to use data to benefit their organization. Built around information submitted by a wide variety of foundations and development offices in both the United States and Canada, the benchmarking database allows development leaders to measure an organization's performance against any peer group—from all foundations who submitted data to organizations with similar revenue, bed size or other metrics.

Using the benchmarking service, philanthropy organizations can access and track key pieces of information, to include:

• specific, customizable reports, including five-year trends
• performance metrics by program
• giving by constituency
• activity tracking for major, annual and planned giving, and events

TRACKING QUALIFIED ACTIVITY

It is important to track individual and collective progress for meaningful activities. Tracking should be aligned with not only the outcomes the organization expects to achieve but also with the organization's processes for achieving those outcomes.

For many organizations, the core process for portfolio management is a multi-step process that involves identifying, engaging, cultivating, soliciting and stewarding donors. Making this process meaningful to your philanthropy team and donors is ESSENTIAL to success. Having all team members (staff and board members) follow a consistent process is very important.

Ensuring the solicitation process is permission-based is vital to success. Obviously, each philanthropic gift advisor has her own personality and communication style; however, the team always asks the same permission-based questions of the donor while moving through the process. This ensures the philanthropic gift advisor and the donor are on the same page. Following the process, the team develops a shared language to ensure the donor drives the conversations, and the philanthropy team actively listens to feedback. Remember, this work is always about the donor's engagement and passion for the mission and how he wants to support the work the organization does to help others.

Without professionally-driven development activity, analyzing financial metrics is putting the cart before the horse.

When utilizing the core process, there are established visit and solicit metrics with weekly, monthly and annual accountabilities. As a foundation, achieving visit and solicit goals ensures a 95% chance of realizing annual financial goals. It is amazing.

By tracking visit activity within the core process in real time—monthly review is preferred—it provides ample feedback as to whether the team is actively visiting prospects according to established metrics. Most successful organizations target completing 6 to 8 face-to-face visits per week per philanthropic gift advisor. With that level of commitment in mind, completion of each call will require the following:

- · 30 minutes preparation time to conduct research and create talking points
- · 1 hour travel time to and from the meeting
- · 1 hour face-to-face meeting
- · 1 hour to follow up and to arrange next steps with the donor
- · 30 minutes for meeting notes and to enter information in the database
- · 1 hour extra time to address other issues

So, estimate each meeting requires four to five hours for planning, prep, execution and follow-up. This means eight meetings per week should take about 40 total hours. At four hours per meeting, completing eight calls would require 32 hours, which leaves eight hours for other assignments. There is some flexibility in this model. It is also recommended to establish metrics on a 10-month year, so annual totals for visits will be 240-320 per year; this allows flexibility for times of the year when donors are less available due to holidays, vacation travel, etc. The key is to empower philanthropy professionals to be out of the office and face-to-face with donors. A lack of focus or assigning philanthropy professionals too many other assignments will impact results.

The organization should also track each philanthropic gift advisor's major solicitations each month. While the gift amount associated with a gift of significance will change based on the organization, the depth of its major gift program, local wealth and other factors, the principal of ensuring a focus on investment-level giving is of the greatest importance here. That said, this should represent approximately two solicitations per month per philanthropic gift advisor, depending on the maturity of the organization's prospect pipeline.

These simple tracking tools help determine if the team has enough meaningful contact with donors within the defined core process and if they are soliciting frequently enough.

In a high performing foundation, 70% to 80% or more of total dollars are being generated by major and planned gifts. However, regardless of the organization's blend of revenue (major gifts, planned gifts, events, employee giving, annual fund and grants), it is important to track a list of potential donors for major gifts and planned giving. Tracking a list of donors who are already engaged within the core process is vital to help set annual financial goals for major gifts and planned gifts.

In setting goals based on relationships already being developed within the core process, it is important to know what the conversion rate has been when soliciting major commitments. The conversion rate is the percentage of gift commitments secured relative to gift solicitations made. The conversion rate will change over time based upon economic and other factors; however, well-functioning organizations that adhere to a core process can expect a conversion rate of 1 in 2 (50%) or 1 in 3 (33%) with prospects that demonstrate high interest in the "cultivation" and "solicitation" stages. Using the more conservative 33% conversion rate means a gift officer would need a donor pipeline valued at $3 million or more to raise $1 million. For predictive modeling, leaders want to avoid being too top heavy, for example, having only 3 prospects at $1 million each and hoping one donor on that list will make the gift. There are gift table models that demonstrate various ways to approach the gifts needed to reach an annual or campaign goals. One model roughly defines that the organization's "Top 10" donors should account for 50 to 55% of the overall campaign. However, it is worth noting that leaders must be thoughtful in interpreting these numbers, since too high a conversion rate might indicate gifts are being solicited for too low a dollar amount.

Actively monitoring a donor pipeline by quarter and sharing this with the team is a great way to track financial performance as well as activity needed to be successful. Update the list every few weeks to help the team see momentum or lack of momentum. Having two quarters available to view at one time is helpful. Then, update the pipeline with results of the solicitations—and include dollar amounts. In some cases, philanthropy professionals will move a donor from first quarter (Q1) to third quarter (Q3) as they gather more information on timing of the solicitation, so there is also value at looking at the timeline of proposed activities.

The main takeaway here is to use predictive modeling to set goals based on donors currently engaged in the core process. Share this information with the philanthropy team, so they can track it, as well. Confidentiality of these reports is critical to protect donor information related to potential gift amounts being discussed.

MEASURING OUTPUT

Once the philanthropy organization becomes agile at measuring activity within a defined core process that generates visits, demonstrates an appropriate number of solicitations and shows "inputs" tracking at the level needed—it's time to look at outcomes around financial performance.

ENGAGEMENT TIP

Publish a monthly financial report to share overall performance with board members and interested donors. Transparency is important and builds trust. Financial reports should list multiple beneficiaries (hospitals, institutes, etc.) along the top row and then within their columns list the Goal (YTD), the Actual (YTD) and Year End Goal (YEG) for each revenue line: major gifts, planned giving, events, employee giving, annual fund and grants. Whether the organization has one beneficiary or a dozen beneficiaries, this is a great report for foundation board members, health care organization executives and the philanthropy team to review. Being transparent with this financial information helps promote critical conversations about performance and at times motivates board members, health care executives and the philanthropy team to higher accountability for results.

Donors and hospital leadership want to know the philanthropy organization is efficient and that contributions are being used for the intended purpose. Cost ratios for fund development activity vary widely from hospital to hospital and health care system to health care system; however, the philanthropy executive and foundation board can set appropriate standards to achieve based on the organization.

Several common financial metrics utilized in health care philanthropy include:

Return on Investment (ROI) — A key measure that represents the financial return on each dollar spent raising funds during the reporting year. It is also the inverse of the CTRD metric. ROI is an indicator of development effectiveness, illustrating the amount applied toward the bottom line, in relation to the cost. ROI is the product of dividing gross funds raised by total development expenses.

Cost to Raise a Dollar (CTRD) — A key measure of development efficiency, providing an abbreviated look at the total amount spent to raise each dollar in support of the organization's mission. It is the number achieved by dividing development expenses by gross funds raised during the reporting year.

Net Fundraising Returns — An important metric that reflects bottom-line development returns in support of the organization's mission. It is commonly described as the "what" that accompanies the "how" provided by CTRD and ROI. It is the number achieved by subtracting development expenses from gross development revenues from production.

What do these lagging financial indicators say about the organization? Is the organization efficient in raising dollars? What is the Cost to Raise a Dollar (CTRD)? What is the Return on Investment (ROI)? What is total production? It's a good idea to establish organizational

Good Financial Practices to Support Your Journey:

- Share monthly development totals with board members and team.

- Have annual financials audit by accredited/independent accounting firm. and share all audit findings and recommendations.

- Involve board members and major donors in reviewing how dollars are spent and outcomes, so you can celebrate impact.

- Have clearly written major and planned gift agreements that clearly reflect donor intent and include the donor's signature.

- Follow AHP Donor Bill of Rights.

- Acknowledge Gifts in 24/48 hours. Ensure gifts are credited to appropriate accounts. Have finance and gift advisors partner to review restricted funds and to verify dollars have been placed in appropriate accounts.

- Finance and philanthropic gift advisors meet with health care executives responsible for expenditure of funds at least quarterly to ensure funds are expended in a timely fashion and for the appropriate purpose.

- Have control process in place for the release and expenditure of all contributions to ensure compliance with donor intent. Ensure appropriate executives from different departments (finance, foundation leadership, department leadership) sign off on all expenses of $5,000 or greater to ensure accuracy and accountability. More signatures required by higher-level executives for higher 6- and 7- figure expenditures.

- Follow reasonable expenditures on stewardship/recognition, and do not exceed accepted rate of 1.5% to 2.5% of gift value. Most donors do not want the organization to spend large amounts of money to say thank you.

- Invest donor dollars for endowments, gift annuities, etc., prudently and transparently and involve your board members in oversight of these funds.

- Avoid conflicts of interest with all auditing or oversight of funds. Independence of auditors and board oversight committee is critical. Conduct a board vote on all investments, with multiple investment companies interviewed before voting. Monitor investment returns monthly and ensure brokerage firm contract is reviewed at least annually.

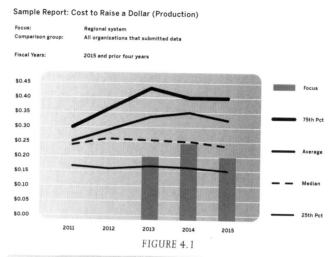

Sample Report: Cost to Raise a Dollar (Production)

Focus: Regional system
Comparison group: All organizations that submitted data

Fiscal Years: 2015 and prior four years

FIGURE 4.1

	Focus Org	Comparison group			
		25th Pct	Median	75th Pct	Average
2011		$0.17	$0.23	$0.30	$0.25
2012		$0.16	$0.26	$0.36	$0.29
2013	$0.20	$0.17	$0.26	$0.42	$0.33
2014	$0.24	$0.17	$0.25	$0.40	$0.34
2015	$0.20	$0.15	$0.23	$0.40	$0.32

FIGURE 4.2

targets for some of these key metrics. The median CTRD in fiscal year 2015 was $0.23, according to the 2016 Association for Healthcare Philanthropy (AHP) Report on Giving - USA. (In Canada, the median CTRD was nearly the same, at $0.24.) Establishing the CTRD goal at or below the median pushes the organization to focus on activities with a low cost to raise a dollar (and, thus, a high return on investment). According to data from the AHP Performance Benchmarking service, major gifts ($0.13 median) and planned giving ($0.08) have the lowest cost to raise a dollar. Centering development strategy around these activities can offset the expense of higher-CTRD activities like special events and acquisition direct mail.

When establishing metrics, consider using a three-year rolling average of performance to track and report efficiency metrics. This

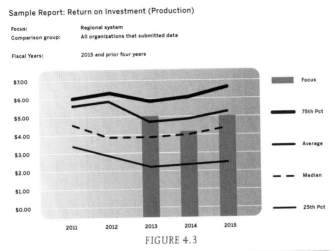

Sample Report: Return on Investment (Production)

| Focus: | Regional system |
| Comparison group: | All organizations that submitted data |

Fiscal Years: 2015 and prior four years

FIGURE 4.3

	Focus Org	Comparison group			
		25th Pct	Median	75th Pct	Average
2011		$3.40	$4.39	$5.97	$5.61
2012		$2.80	$3.94	$6.27	$5.72
2013	$4.99	$2.39	$3.83	$5.75	$4.56
2014	$4.09	$2.51	$3.95	$6.09	$4.81
2015	$5.01	$2.51	$4.29	$6.60	$5.21

FIGURE 4.4

minimizes the effect a single, large, outlier gift can have on results. Landing a big gift can make metrics look great one year, but failing to secure a gift of comparable size the following year creates a year-to-year seesaw effect that may misrepresent the philanthropy organization's effectiveness.

When tracking performance, it is helpful to compare the organization to others in the industry to get an objective sense of performance relative to peer organizations. The AHP Benchmarking Service is an example of comparative data on peers in health care philanthropy. No matter where the organization is on its path to excellence, maintaining discipline to track, report and share objective information with the philanthropy team, foundation board members, donors and health care executives is very important. Being transparent and metric driven is essential to improving results. Tracking and comparing financial performance to other hospitals can help the organization improve by highlighting what is working— and what is not. Peer organizations are often willing to share best practices and how they achieved successful results. Having baseline financial performance is the first solid step in a performance journey.

Financially-based metrics provide an important feedback loop to determine how effective fund development efforts have been and to analyze the effectiveness of the team. Just remember, financial performance looks backward at the road the organization has already traveled. There are lessons and important insights to garner from this information, but progress is rarely built on looking in the rearview mirror. Actively promoting the mission and vision and asking people to invest in the future is the forward-looking perspective.

CONCLUSION

Information is power. Providing information on the inputs and outputs of your performance will spark engagement and commit-

VALUABLE FINANCE METRICS

Here is a list of other financial metrics to track on your journey to high performance.

• Pledge Fulfillment Rate—Track what percentage of major donors fulfill pledge commitments. 95% or higher fulfillment should be a goal.

• Relevant financial information provide regular quarterly disclosures of foundation's financials (both development production counting method and GAAP) to foundation board and health care organization executives.

• Results from benchmarking studies—The Association for Healthcare Philanthropy Performance Benchmarking Service provides industry-relevant information. Compare your results and best practices with others to improve performance.

ment to high performance. While sharing this information can be intimidating when performance is not good, it does provide a starting point for improvement. While mission will always be core to all aspects of work, it is time to take the "mystery" out of fund development and embrace the critical measurements that drive high performance. Sharing key inputs and outputs demonstrates to foundation boards, hospital executives and the philanthropy team that there is a process that can be measured and improved upon year after year to achieve critical philanthropy objectives. A metric-driven approach shows leaders the mission-driven philanthropy organization is committed to maximizing financial performance. Embracing metrics and financial accountability, keeping work goals simple and clear and never taking your eye off the mission means philanthropic dollars will follow.

KEYS TO SUCCESS

1. Once you embrace a relentless focus on mission, engage people who share the passion for your mission to get involved and keep your ego and self-interest out of it. What would you say your top three to five strategic goals should look like?

2. Let the foundation be the "storyteller" of the mission. Bring the mission to life! Share that story with everyone. Have a case for giving that succinctly identifies three to five major priorities that will help your organization fulfill your mission's promise.

3. Follow a standardized core process for engaging donors. Train your team to always follow that process. They should actively identify and engage donors in supporting your mission.

4. Create a foundation team environment that "lives the mission" daily and emphasizes that staff collaborate to put the donor at the center of your mission-based focus. (It is not about staff promotions, hierarchy, office politics or a dozen other distractions you could encounter.)

5. Create active, engaged, community-led, volunteer, development boards to be ambassadors and advocates for your mission.

CHAPTER 5

Implementing a Strategic Information Management Environment

Christopher M. Cannon, CFRE

A "strategic information management environment" is essential for high-performing health care philanthropy teams. This environment is an aggregation of data resources and related functions integrated for the purposes of supporting philanthropy. In information systems terminology, such an environment allows an organization to gather, store, maintain, process and analyze its data. For philanthropy, the notion is similar and the environment addresses the essential question: "How should an organization handle its data to help raise money and build relationships?" A great environment includes talented team members, useful technology, smooth business processes, timely reporting and accurate and complete data. This chapter examines the foundation of this environment—data—and presents a coherent approach to implementing strategic information management in any health care philanthropy organization.

FUNDAMENTALS FIRST

Great philanthropy shops start with great data. Without great data, reports are wrong, processes are clunky, technology is useless and talented staff are hampered by incomplete information. Every philanthropy professional should understand enough about data to help implement a strategic information management environment.

Fuel for Fundraising

This approach—starting with data—is obvious and yet can be counterintuitive in the fund development organization. It is obvious because the world in general and health care in particular are increasingly data-driven. Philanthropy professionals often hear "big data" is uncovering behavioral patterns and "social data" is identifying new potential donors. Whether through sophisticated analytics or simple contact data, data is essential to philanthropy. However, the value of having more data and more sophisticated analyses is also counterintuitive because philanthropy results are increasingly coming from a smaller number of donors. For example, Giving USA's 2016 results showed more than $390 billion was given, yet just 18 donors contributed about $4.3 billion, per a January 7, 2017, Forbes article. So, which is it? Does our industry need more and more data or will it rely on fewer and fewer big donors? The answer, of course, is both. A strategic information management environment will help leverage both trends through focusing attention on top constituents while automating as much as possible to maintain data for the entire constituent pool.

Every organization must start by building its basic data first. It is critical to have shared definitions in place when evaluating the fundamentals. Every organization should have a "data dictionary" that spells out how data points are defined. For example, for this chapter, "constituent" means the individuals or organizations involved with an "organization," which means a health care philanthropy entity. If your organization does not have a shared set of definitions for data, misinterpretation will diminish the effectiveness of the strategic information environment, particularly in the area of reporting. The Association for Healthcare Philanthropy has created a set of definitional standards with its AHP Standards Manual. In addition, information management policies should be documented and applied. These policies, including a data standards document and a data use policy, will guide the organization's strategic information management environment. For example, a strategic information management environment will address issues around HIPAA-compliant data gathering, storage, access and use by philanthropy programs.

Biographical and Contact Data

With definitions in place, an organization seeking to gather better data should start with biographical and contact data. Biographical and contact data points are the building blocks for all other aspects of a strategic information management environment. These are the simplest data points but not always the easiest. For example, "constituent name" is a piece of biographical data that can be tricky. Without "gender," it cannot be determined if a constituent named "Chris" is male or female. In addition, in health care, knowing if one is a physician is important and the "title" and "suffix" depend on having this information. Hence, creating a "Chris Smith" constituent record presents immediate challenges without more complete data. Similar nuances are important to tackle related to titles and suffixes. As mundane as this seems, sending a "Dear Mrs. Jones" letter to Dr. Jones may well make her less likely to donate. These little things matter. A strategic information management environment would help an organization establish protocols to address issues like this one. In turn, the environment would strengthen the organization's ability to build a relationship.

After handling name field nuances, other biographical data points need attention because they affect philanthropy. Birthdate and deceasing information are necessary and useful for certain programs, particularly gift planning. Knowing a constituent's business(es) or employer and position is essential for prospecting and relationship management. An organization needs to detail what is important and build the environment to support gathering these data points.

Contact data points are equally essential. These include mailing address, phone number, email address and social media links. Without these, constituent relationships fizzle. For North American-based organizations, mailing address information is largely available for constituents and is easily maintained using tested products from the U.S. Postal Service and third parties. Email addresses and phone numbers are increasingly valuable for philanthropy purposes. Great shops are discerning primary email addresses from secondary addresses; that is, they are learning which email addresses their constituents actually open. Top organizations are also actively seeking cell phone and business phone numbers to increase contact rates, as home phone usage is waning.

Social data management is the newest contact data consideration for organizations. A constituent's Facebook, Instagram, LinkedIn or Twitter account can provide substantial insights into the constituent's interests, relationships and potential engagement with the institution. These channels are increasingly serving as a contact and communication point for constituents. In particular, social data management can help an organization address the trend of users favoring instant messaging. Many constituents may exclude health care organizations from their communications via this channel but capturing those that will engage via instant message is important and will be growing in the years to come.

For health care philanthropy, the biographical data "basics" are broader due to HIPAA-compliant access to patient information. Biographical and contact information about an organization's patients and guarantors is available and acceptable to gather and maintain. Additional data points about the patient's experience can also be

Consider this: you have a great potential prospect who has given three, $1,000 gifts to your organization in the last year, but you have no phone number or email on the prospect's record. What do you do? Perhaps research can locate a contact point. Perhaps you write a letter and hope for the best. Perhaps you move to the next prospect that is easier to contact. What you need is an environment that prioritizes certain data—finding this prospect's phone number—over other less valuable pieces of data. In such an environment, the team would prioritize finding a business, cell or home phone number once the first $1,000 is received, with email and other contact points prioritized slightly lower, allowing the organization to improve stewardship and communication earlier. If Google does not yield this information readily, consider seeking advice from the Association of Professional Researchers for Advancement (aprahome.org), which leads the industry in internet and other research, analysis and prospect development techniques.

collected. While grateful patient information is an area that requires more focus than can be provided here, these data points should be part of the strategic information management environment.

Interaction and Outcome Data

Interaction and outcome data points are those associated with how and when an organization engages its constituents and vice-versa. This includes the all-important giving records, action and solicitation activities, volunteerism, direct response efforts, event invitations and participation, membership and donor society levels, online engagement such as "open" indicators and "likes" on Facebook and other types of interaction. These are the data points that show how a constituent is involved with an organization and how representatives from the organization have approached the constituent.

The more consistent and complete these data points are, the stronger the strategic information management environment will be. Coding will be more clear. Trends will be more evident. Data will be more trusted. Reports will be more effective. It is imperative that an organization spend the time and energy necessary to collect, maintain and standardize interaction and outcome data, because this is the primary source of reporting and analysis.

These data are also harder to standardize across health care organizations. Due to resource differences, larger shops will have access to certain data that smaller shops do not. Some organizations have deeper data gathering processes for online engagement or prospect management than others. The trick is that no matter an organization's size and complexity, interaction and outcome data are essential to effective fund development and, as such, must be part of the strategic information management environment. Gift and pledge data regarding date, amount and fund are among the "must-have" data points, although details per contribution can vary. Solicitation strategy data points should be part of the strategic information management plan, including some indicator of direct response appeals (i.e., mailings sent, emails delivered, solicitation calls made) and planned solicitations for larger gifts, yet the details for these can and will vary considerably.

> It is imperative that an organization spend the time and energy necessary to collect, maintain and standardize interaction and outcome data, because this is the primary source of reporting and analysis.

The fundamental point for all health care philanthropy teams is that policies and practices for gathering and managing interaction and outcome data are essential. Like much of development work, these data points are driven mostly by disciplined behavior. The actual codes in place, database used and reports generated matter less than the daily, constituent data gathering necessary. The good news is that automation of data entry, pre-determined online engagement user journeys, text-to-speech applications and other tools are making this work easier; yet, no technology will replace the act of an individual philanthropic gift advisor recording her efforts.

Strategy and Analysis Data Points

Strategy and analysis data points are very useful for philanthropy, yet tend to vary even more than interaction data points. Strategy and analysis data points are those associated with how an organization categorizes and analyzes constituent information to build philanthropic strategies. These data points are often created by the organization or a third-party to reflect "ratings" for capacity and inclination to give. The primary data points focus on solicitation plans, typically called "proposals" or "opportunities." "Analytics" data also falls in this category. The scores generated from statistical analysis of an organization's constituents largely come from the organization's data. Organizations can expect their strategy and analysis results to be better where they have deeper and broader data available per constituent. As such, these data points are really a result of a sound foundation of data fundamentals. That is, an organization cannot get fancy with, say, statistical regression analysis until it has the fundamentals in place.

PRINCIPLES FOR THE STRATEGIC INFORMATION MANAGEMENT ENVIRONMENT

Once essential data points are in place, organizations should build a data environment that leverages great data to increase philanthropy results. All data points are not equal. Data must be prioritized to direct data gathering toward those data points that matter more. For example, business phone numbers are exceptionally valuable for philanthropic gift advisors as such phone numbers increase the chances of reaching a constituent during the work day. These numbers are also a surrogate for other data details. For example, if you have a work phone number, you likely know where that constituent works and perhaps their position, two very useful pieces of a prospecting plan. Because some data matter more than others, a strategic information management environment should guide the prioritization of constituent records.

Value over Volume

To foster the type of data needed for great philanthropic operations, the organization should first emphasize the value of certain records over the typical constituent record. Figure 5.1 illustrates the reality that some records have more value than others and warrant more attention. For example, updating mailing addresses for all donors is useful and reflects high volume data management activities, particularly where a high percentage of those updates are automated. However, making certain that, say, board members' addresses are always up to date is much more valuable to the organization for at least two reasons. First, board members are often the organization's best donors, so having accurate and complete addresses ensures we can engage these individuals. Second, our board members' perceptions of our operations often start with data issues. Many philanthropy operations audits start as "$50 problems;" that is, a small issue such as using the wrong salutation on a board member's receipt may lead to significant concerns over confidence and systems integrity. Cleaner, better data environments give board members confidence in our efforts; poor, ineffective data suggests the organization is not performing optimally.

As Figure 5.1 indicates, an organization should provide an increasing amount of attention to records that have higher levels of strategic value. Typically, "value" is defined as a function of past giving and future potential giving. The value of relationships and connections should also be considered, as should organizational value from key stakeholders. Teams should first focus where the value of records is high and the number of records under consideration is relatively low. Where the volume of data is highest, increased automation should be implemented.

Increased Attention

FIGURE 5.1: *Focusing on Value over Volume*

Front-of-the-Line Protocols

High value data should be a part of a "front-of-the-line" protocol. Team members would follow this protocol in handling all data related to "front-of-the-line" constituents. An organization would create a grouping of constituents that reflect their relatively high value. Top donors would be in the group, as would top volunteers and leaders. Potential donors of a certain level, or perhaps those assigned to a philanthropic gift advisor, would be in the "front-of-the-line" group. In many organizations, physicians and staff are included, particularly when these constituents are also donors. The resulting group of most valued constituents is often less than 10% of the organization's constituent database count. With this group, special gift administration steps are taken and specific practices for updating records with new addresses, phone numbers and other updates are applied. Automation of updates to these records is often more carefully reviewed or updates are handled one-by-one.

A well-implemented "front-of-the-line" approach will leverage the benefits of the well-known "80/20 Rule." Detailed originally by Vilfredo Pareto in an 1896 paper "Cours d'économie politique," the 80/20 Rule states that 80% of the production comes from 20% of the resources. In philanthropy terms, this suggests at least 80% of the dollars comes from 20% of the donors. This ratio—80/20—is a good predictor of the ratio of giving a small number of donors provide to organization's philanthropy production each year. The 80/20 Rule also supports the rationale behind having a "front-of-the-line" approach, as most organizations find that only a fraction of their donors provide the vast majority of their giving on an annual basis. The "front-of-the-line" approach allows organizations to focus more time and attention on their best. When used within a strategic information management environment, the results are high levels of detailed focus on and management of the organization's best constituents and efficient and effective automation in managing the organization's high-volume data and processes.

Many philanthropy teams have de facto "front-of-the-line" practices. However, too often, these practices are reactive rather than proactively operationalized in everyday work flows. For example, when a generous check is delivered to the gift administration team, heightened, sometimes anxious, attention is placed on processing the gift. Strategic information management environments place extra attention on such events, but do so in a carefully planned, universally understood and shared protocol that courses through the entire team. Because of the specialized attention to these details, such protocols are similar to the increased services one might experience as a private or executive banking client versus being a run-of-the-mill big bank customer. More resources, checks and balances are added to reflect the value of the engagement and potential for future business, so to speak. Not all constituents will qualify for such services in the same way not all bank customers will receive the same attention as private banking clients.

Balance Accuracy, Speed and Volume

Best-in-class data environments must also balance the countervailing forces of accuracy, speed and volume. Expectations for accuracy, for example, are directly tied to how quickly data management steps can be taken. The greater the expectation for accuracy, the slower the data updates will likely be. The slower data management processes are, the less volume can be handled. The less volume is handled, the less accurate the data becomes over time.

It is a difficult balance to strike. Successful organizations typically manage this conundrum by automating as much as possible without jeopardizing front-of-the-line data and related processes. Special processes are adopted that identify vital records and ensure all team members provide careful and thorough attention when handling these records.

Philanthropy professionals strive to treat all constituents with respect. This data strategy is less about respecting marginally engaged constituents and more about focusing limited resources at the top of the donor pyramid.

This means, for example, functions like conducting a national change of address (NCOA) update via the U.S. Postal Service are automated to a point, with a one-by-one review of any front-of-the-line records prior to updating those records.

On the other side of this balancing act is the substantial volume of constituent records that matter very little to the organization's total impact and production. This is a difficult point to concede, but it is a verifiable fact: some constituents matter much more than others. The mechanics of philanthropy must follow the two golden rules. The first, of course, is to "do unto others as you would like done to you." The second is less egalitarian: "he or she who has the gold makes the rules." Strategic information management environments support both rules. First, the organization should handle as much data as possible with the end in mind, which is often that a constituent now may become a donor in a decade or two or three. Second, a "front-of-the-line" approach will ensure the data for the organization's best donors are carefully managed.

Streamlined organizations adopt an approach whereby automation is the only potential source of data management for marginal constituents with very little giving and no recent activity. Philanthropy professionals strive to treat all constituents with respect. This data strategy is less about respecting marginally engaged constituents and more about focusing limited resources at the top of the donor pyramid. As a result, organizations should develop a tolerance for occasional errors and issues among the bottom portion of the constituent base. This point is critical to balancing the often crushing volume of potential data points with the speed and levels of accuracy required. Expectations for all three aspects—accuracy, speed and volume—should be codified and become part of the organization's metrics for success. In doing so, organizations should build in some realistic, allowable level of inaccuracy.

OPERATIONALIZING THE ENVIRONMENT

With fundamental data elements and key principles in place, organizations should operationalize a strategic information management environment in four steps. Data management is like shoveling sand on the beach: it is repetitive and can be hard to maintain. Therefore, it is important to establish an environment on a solid foundation, starting with accurate and complete data.

Step 1: Gather and maintain the data.

An organization should catalog its data points and document how data is managed over time. This should include the obvious bio-demographic and contact data points, outcome data points and strategic and analytic data points. An organization may also have some unique data needs that shape what is gathered. Once data points are in place, the environment can start to take shape around it.

STRATEGIC INFORMATION MANAGEMENT

Step 2: Adopt strategic information environment principles and policies

An organization should commit to the essential elements of great data management. The right data should be valued by providing more attention to these points and automating less important data management. In addition, organization-wide policies for data integrity, maintenance and use are important to prepare for ongoing data management needs.

Step 3: Establish the truth about the data

An organization should establish a baseline for what its data actually includes. The list can be long, but a handful of core questions tend to suffice: How many constituent records are there? How many are individuals? Deceased? Married, with spouse information? Potential duplicates? Donors? How many constituents can we mail? Email? Call? What do we know about constituents' employment, relationships and interests? How do the numbers look for the "front-of-the-line" group? This becomes the basis for comparison for future improvements.

Step 4: Maintain and refine the environment

With data in place, principles shared and a baseline set, an organization should seek to constantly improve upon its data to support increased philanthropy efforts. Data append projects for employer and title information, cell phones, social media handles and other frequent gaps in the data should be filled in when there is a clear business need. In addition to expanding strategic information, the fundamentals will need consistent attention. A data health calendar, as depicted in Figure 5.2, is a valuable tool to keep maintenance items on track.

Sample Data Management Calendar

Type of Data Management Work	Jan	Feb	Mar	Apr	May	Jun	Jul	Aug	Sep	Oct	Nov	Dec
Physician/Employee Load	X	X	X	X	X	X	X	X	X	X	X	X
Grateful Patient Load	X	X	X	X	X	X	X	X	X	X	X	X
Front-of-the-Line Coding Review	X	X	X	X	X	X	X	X	X	X	X	X
Donor Honor Roll Data Review	X	X	X	X	X	X	X	X	X	X	X	X
Quality Control Query Review	X	X	X			X	X	X	X			
Lost Constituent Research									X			X
Phone Research*						X	X	X				
Email Research*						X	X	X				
Social Media Handle Updates* (vendor)		X	X		X							
Address Updates, aka NCOA (vendor)	X			X			X			X		
Phone and Email Append (vendor)										X	X	
Deceased Append (vendor)									X			
Employer/Business Title (vendor)									X	X		
External Wealth Screening (vendor)			X	X								

*indicates efforts should be aimed at front-of-the-line constituents

FIGURE 5.2: Sample Data Calendar Illustrates Which Data to Focus on and When

APPROACHES TO ASSESSING AND REFINING THE DATA ENVIRONMENT

Once an organization has operationalized a strategic information management environment, periodic assessment and refinement will be necessary. This is "step 4" in the environment ramp-up; and it deserves special attention because strategic information management requires ongoing, careful and thorough administration. These considerations for evaluating the data environment apply to all stages of implementing and, then, maintaining an effective data environment.

Perception versus reality

Philanthropy professionals' data environment expectations are typically pretty high. Part of this is a misunderstanding of the volume in play. Part of this is a misunderstanding of the time and energy available to deliver high quality data. A common theme about data expectations has borne out: philanthropy professionals' perceptions of the data are often worse than the reality of the data. Closing the gap between perceptions of data and the reality is an important step toward properly evaluating the current state of the environment. For example, many philanthropy professionals believe their organizations suffer from significant duplicate records. Even in those cases where this may be true (where perhaps 3% or more of a database appears to be a duplicate record), it is likely duplicate record issues have little impact on philanthropy results. If a "front-of-the-line" approach is taken toward potential duplicate records, such an issue tends to be a mere cost of doing business. Instead of "shoveling more sand" to get the potential duplicate record count to zero, great strategic information management shops shrink the gap between perception and reality, increasing trust in and use of data in the process.

Anecdotal versus Systemic Issues

Data environments are rife with anecdotal issues. Many of those aforementioned "$50 problems" are one-off errors or oversights that should not reflect on the whole system—except they do. Misinterpretation is a frequent contributor to issues. This is why shared definitions and a baseline expectation for accuracy are so important in a strategic information management environment.

There are three core issues that plague data integrity and need attention:

- errors
- omissions, and
- timing.

Perhaps there is a real error in the data, such as a misspelling of a name. Perhaps there is an omission of data, such as the lack of a spouse name resulting in an inaccurate receipt. Perhaps the timing of a data point is out-of-date. In each of these cases, organizations evaluating the data environment should establish acceptable levels of each sort of issue. For errors, nearly none should be expected on front-of-the-line records but those constituents at the bottom of the pyramid may suffer more than desired. So long as the issues minimally affect philanthropy results, organizations need to build a tolerance for some level of error. For omissions, the same front-of-the-line logic may apply, with an emphasis on getting names, phones numbers and email addresses right, so constituents can be engaged and solicited. For timing issues, a disciplined data health calendar can help minimize the impact (*See Figure 5.2*).

In all of these issues, systemic problems must be addressed as quickly and thoroughly as possible. Frequent errors by a staff member should be managed. Inaccurate data fields used in reports or through mail-merge functions on donor receipts should be re-programmed. Omissions of key data points on a broad set of constituent records should be resolved through data appends from trusted vendors. Timing issues, such as when data updating lags significantly behind, should also be systematically resolved through a complete data management calendar. In all of these cases, it is imperative the organization's definitions, protocols and baselines inform the whole team about what is within a normal range and, therefore, is acceptable to support the team's philanthropy efforts.

Impact versus Frequency

Timing plays another role in building a strong data environment in the form of frequency of issues. In many cases, we remember the anecdotal, one-time scenario very distinctly as if that scenario were the norm. These issues sometimes become more of those "$50 problems" that receive a great deal of attention and decrease confidence in the data despite having very little impact on actual fund development efforts. The strategic information management environment should be organized to fix such errors while deemphasizing the issue unless if happens too often or has a truly significant impact. Figure 5.3 from An Executive Guide to Fundraising Operations highlights how to evaluate an organization's data management issues.[1] If they are infrequent or insignificant, best-in-class organizations ignore them. Mistakes happen. However, if the "front-of-the-line" is affected or the volume suggests a systematic problem, an organization should immediately resolve the issue.

For errors, nearly none should be expected on front-of-the-line records but those constituents at the bottom of the pyramid may suffer more than desired. So long as the issues minimally affect philanthropy results, organizations need to build a tolerance for some level of error.

NEXT PRACTICES

Innovations in health care philanthropy occur rapidly. Grateful patient programs, third-party events, peer-to-peer giving, shifting industry demands and priorities, changes in federal programs and funding and other catalysts are shaping fund development efforts, which in turn are shaping what data are needed to advance philan-

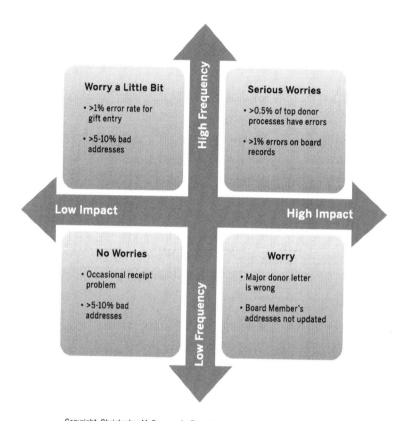

FIGURE 5.3:*Weighing the Impact and Frequency of Data Management Issues*

thropy. A strategic information management environment should prepare an organization for such innovations, yet it can be challenging to predict and prepare for the future.

Once the fundamentals of data and the principles of a strategic information management environment are adopted and embedded in an organization's development approach, new and neat data-related strategies can be considered. These areas tend to focus on the "why" and "how" of decision-making. That is, information is coupled with an understanding of what to do next. This area of data management is often called "data science" in the industry, and the

88

work overlaps a great deal with "prospect development" techniques and strategies in philanthropy.

Best practices for these innovative approaches to strategic information management are useful to explore, yet the result of benchmarking with the most innovative analytics shops in health care may often prove overwhelming to the typical shop. It is often better for organizations to adopt "practices that are best." That is, no matter what neat, new things are popular at the moment, what is right for an organization will vary by the organization's size, history, constituent base and other factors. A few trends are likely here to stay and should further inform an organization's strategic information management:

Analytics

Analytics involves the practice of applying statistical techniques to data to improve prediction or projections. Large shops likely will need dedicated staff to use machine learning from data to build models for giving behavior. Smaller shops can benefit from analytics, perhaps through employing vendors or conducting periodic projects. These can be as simple as creating a "score" for constituents based on the presence or absence of data.

Social data management

Constituents are increasingly active on social media channels, producing insights into the constituent's interests and connections. Gathering these data points (sometimes referred to as "scraping" or perhaps obtained through a vendor's product) can be useful. However, the process can be tedious, so a plan is needed for how the results will be leveraged.

Third-party efforts and constituent development

Constituent-driven, peer-to-peer fund development can be effective for health care philanthropy, yet it creates challenges for data management. Data integrity challenges due to constituent entry choices, errors and volume challenges when peer-to-peer efforts expand require special attention. A strategic information management environment should be set up to handle these issues, yet it is important to remember the delicate balance between accuracy, speed and volume when new, data-intensive efforts arise.

CONCLUSION

Health care philanthropy requires great data. Exactly what "great" means, which "data" and "how" and "why" remain relatively idiosyncratic to each organization. Some strategic information management fundamentals and principles are universal, yet each philanthropy professional will blend a bit of this data science with her own art to build relationships and to bring in more and more funding. The purpose of implementing a strategic information management environment is that an organization can operationalize its practices for gathering, storing and analyzing the right data and data management practices for its success. At the same time, the organization can optimize what it knows about its constituents and how it leverages its resources to generate the highest levels of support among its constituents. By focusing first on the fundamentals and, then, building an organization-specific environment, every health care philanthropy organization can implement an effective strategic information management environment.

References

1. Christopher Cannon, An Executive's Guide to Fundraising Operations (Hoboken: John Wiley & Sons, 2011).

CHAPTER 6

Advancing Annual Giving Multi-channel Strategies for Pipeline Development

Ann Thompson-Haas, FAHP

Funds raised from annual giving have sustained hospitals, hospices and other health care organizations since the simple collection of alms to provide free beds or services for those unable to pay. Today, annual giving is a multi-faceted, multi-channel and multi-goal component of the comprehensive development program.

Annual giving is shifting rapidly from a primary focus on dollars raised to a shared focus on revenue and donor base development. In this newer paradigm, annual giving includes activities to secure gifts from donors every year, while providing sustaining revenue. Further, annual giving creates a pool of prospective donors for campaign, major and planned gifts.

Specific goals of today's strategic annual giving program are to acquire new donors, build an active base, retain loyal donors and nurture long-term giving relationships. The resulting pipeline of established and engaged donors provides a predictable, measurable stream of annual revenue. In addition, targeted tactics to develop mid-level, high-value annual and consistent givers are used to position select donors for larger, transformational gifts.

The shift in focus from revenue-only to revenue and pipeline development can provide profound outcomes for annual giving and for overall financial results. This transition takes careful planning, a strategic view and, perhaps most of all, discipline.

Modern annual giving strategy integrates channels, such as events and direct response, with targeted activities for donor acquisition, retention and engagement. Advanced analytics measure success and help identify prospective major and planned gift donors. In this multi-faceted approach to annual giving, a strategic information management environment and development staff with data management capacity are essential.

An emphasis on donor development in annual giving is not wholly new. However, many organizations have significant opportunity to reframe and manage their annual giving programs and to achieve the greatest short-term and long-term benefits from a revenue focus coupled with pipeline focus.

DRIVERS AND CHALLENGES OF THE NEW ANNUAL GIVING MODEL

A key driver of the pipeline approach to annual giving is the shift in donor motives and expectations. As the "traditionalist" donor cohort, roughly over age 70, shrinks, the baby boomer group is moving to the forefront. Traditionalists give because it is the right thing to do, while boomers want to see the greatest impact for their gifts. They evaluate a range of charities and decide which ones deserve their loyalty.

Health care organizations can reap benefits over time when they purposefully invest in building loyalty and stewarding donors from their first gifts, to second gifts, to third gifts and beyond. This long-term view may be a challenge for health care executives that, naturally, take a more short-term, revenue-focused view. The successful annual giving professional anticipates this challenge, leads the organization through a transition to the pipeline approach and uses productivity measures to show financial benefit over time.

Fast-evolving technology is another driver of change. More channels, such as email and social media, are available to support donor engagement and gift development. It is tempting to shift solicitation and stewardship to electronic channels to save on cost. However, boomers and even younger health care donors are unpredictable in their responses to various channels – presenting a challenge for planning. For example, hospital donors may respond to email solicitation at a lower rate than other charities, while welcoming electronic newsletters with updates on how gifts are used. Now, it is important to carefully choose channels and track individual donor channel preferences.

Overall competition for annual dollars and donors is growing and is another driver for the changing annual giving paradigm. Donors have decreased the number of charities they support each year. Some individuals have less disposable income to give. Other donors choose to give larger gifts to fewer organizations to make a more meaningful difference.

As a result, many health care organizations find the average life-cycle of giving is approximately two gifts. This trend may make the strongest case for shifting from a revenue-only focus to a loyalty and pipeline focus. A pipeline focus helps expand the natural life-cycle of giving to multiple gifts and leads more donors to make the major or planned gifts that return the highest value to the organization.

Health care organizations must embrace the benefits and challenges of changes in donor behaviors and technology. At the same time, they must design an approach is right for its own constituency and situation.

93

INTEGRATE MULTIPLE CHANNELS TARGETED TO DONOR GROUPS

The range of channels available for annual gift and pipeline development helps grow an active donor base by meeting a range of supporter needs. Community hospitals, children's hospitals, academic medical centers and hospices may choose and use channels in slightly different ways based on the composition and interests of their individual donor groups.

Today's strategic and multi-channel annual giving program emphasizes tools that best fulfill the motivations of the organization's core constituencies. As a result, the long-term pipeline is developed naturally and more cost-effectively.

TRADITIONAL ANNUAL GIVING CHANNELS INCLUDE:
- special events
- direct mail
- commemorative giving
- support groups
- giving circles
- telephone
- monthly giving
- face-to-face personal solicitation

DIGITAL CHANNELS INCLUDE:
- email
- social media
- peer-to-peer solicitation
- text-to-give
- crowdfunding

Annual donors tend to choose their preferred channel of support and give primarily through that channel. For example, special event donors return to events, while rarely giving to a regular direct mail appeal. Their social and community recognition needs are met through their involvement or attendance in the event. Conversely, direct mail donors rarely respond to event invitations.

Long gone are the days when the entire donor base receives every event invitation or appeal asking for a ticket purchase, sponsorship or gift. Now, a multi-channel approach offers a range of giving options and targets those options to groups of donors known or supposed to respond to that channel.

Other channels may be integrated for stewardship and engagement. Multi-channel, therefore, refers to choosing and using channels strategically for both solicitation and engagement. The key to success is building an integrated annual giving strategy by channel, by message purpose and by constituent group.

For example, donors acquired from grateful patient or community mailings may receive thank you phone calls, print stewardship and electronic newsletters placed strategically between mail appeals. A pre-mailing email may prime the pump for a direct mail retention appeal to improve response rate.

Ideally, a 12- to 18-month multi-channel integrated strategy knits together the phone channel and the digital channels for retention touches, while the direct mail responsive donor is asked to renew his or her support through the preferred channel of mail. At the right time and with the right ask, the mail donor may transition to digital giving, while the emphasis initially is to build loyalty by asking for renewal gifts by the same channel through which the initial gift was made.

Top channels of choice vary by organization size, location or type, such as community or children's hospitals. It is important to make strategic decisions about channel use and timing to secure the highest financial or donor development benefit. In particular, avoid keeping traditions that are no longer working, such as events, and avoid adopting tactics simply because they are new and interesting, such as crowdfunding.

The benefits and challenges of various annual giving channels have evolved over the past decades. No single channel provides the silver bullet for building an active donor base and growing income. Best results come from choosing a portfolio of annual giving tools and implementing them diligently over time.

Special events have been a traditional staple for health care annual giving and are an important part of the annual portfolio for many organizations. Events, however, may or may not be a viable tool for developing pipeline. They are labor intensive, and many organizations are discontinuing events to focus staff time on working personally with donors to develop mid-level and high-value annual or major gifts. For this reason, events are being scaled back or used more selectively.

Some organizations find a signature event is essential to engage community members at a higher level than possible without an event. The most successful of these organizations strategically use events to develop relationships with individual attendees and committee members who are qualified major gift prospects.

A top trend is to rigorously evaluate existing events and new event proposals for overall cost benefit, including the opportunity cost of staff involvement. Based on the analysis, strategically transition away from non-productive events and add new events only if they will have a clear revenue and pipeline return on the effort involved.

Direct mail remains a core tactic for health care annual giving, despite shaky response rates. When implemented thoughtfully, mail is a cost-effective way to acquire and engage donors who desire to support the mission without the social aspect of other annual giving tools.

Response rates are slipping, perhaps tied to perceptions resulting from changes in health care delivery and reimbursement. Nevertheless, direct mail is an essential annual giving channel. Response rates and return on investment can be improved with strategic segmentation and by targeting constituents most likely to respond and give long-term.

Support groups and giving circles can provide a framework for today's donors who want hands-on involvement in addition to providing financial support. Support groups can be labor intensive, but provide philanthropic gift advisors the opportunity to engage and develop relationships with group members. Giving circles, such as women's giving groups, continue to grow in popularity. They are slightly more efficient than support groups while offering donors similar opportunities for involvement in the mission and engagement with leadership.

Commemorative gifts, contributions made in memory or honor of others, can help position health care organizations in the minds of the giving community. Commemorative donors are often difficult to move to the second or third gift, however, leading organizations to apply their resources to other strategies.

The use of the telephone in annual giving has changed over time. Most often, the phone has been used to wrap-up a capital campaign by securing multi-year pledges. This same model may or may not work for annual giving.

Other options include using the phone to recapture lapsed donors or to upgrade select donors to giving club levels. For acquisition, it is best to start by testing the concept and then evaluating if donors acquired via the phone become long-term donors.

A stewardship and cultivation phone call can provide benefit when integrated into a comprehensive direct response program. For example, use the phone to make thank you calls to new donors to say "welcome," to call second time donors to say "thank you again" and to reach out to consistent givers to say "thank you for your loyalty."

Engage volunteers to conduct an annual phone "thank-a-thon" to wrap up the current cycle of giving or to kick-off a new annual effort. When possible, take the opportunity in a thank you call to ask questions and learn about the donor's passions, giving interests and preferred channels of communication.

The ongoing development of digital tools is exciting. Annual giving professionals may be tempted to emphasize online channels over other options to save time and expense. As the dust settles on digital options, it appears their effectiveness ranges widely based on use, intended results and type of organization.

Digital channels are often most effective when used to provide stewardship, to reinforce key messages and to support other fund development channels, such as events, raffles and support groups. It is critical to make the right choices about how to use and integrate digital options.

ANN THOMPSON-HAAS, FAHP

CAREFULLY INTEGRATE AND MANAGE DIGITAL CHANNELS

The use of digital channels deserves close examination. Without question, the world is going digital. In the business world, companies thrive when they master the digital mix. In the nonprofit world, best approaches are still evolving while the time is right to develop a long-term digital annual giving strategy.

As with all of annual giving, an organization's strategy begins with an in-depth understanding of its constituents and their likely online behavior. How many prefer to give online? How many go online to support their decision to give while giving through the mail or event attendance? How many will read a piece of mail and then go online to make a gift?

This cross-channel behavior is similar to consumer purchasing. One customer may see an item in a print direct mail catalogue and order the item from company's web site for home delivery. Another may see the item in the catalogue and visit the store to complete the purchase. A third customer may solely engage digitally and purchase online, perhaps even on her mobile device. An integrated annual giving strategy integrates the digital channel in the same way and allows donors to choose their preferences.

The effectiveness of online options also varies by type of organization and purpose. For example, children's hospitals are a more natural match for email solicitation, text-to-give and peer-to-peer fundraising. Community hospitals often use email, targeted web sites, social media, and peer-to-peer fundraising tied to special events or campaigns. Even when community hospital donors do not choose to make gifts online, engaging donors through digital channels can strengthen donor attachment to the mission.

The best approach is to test and determine what works for use of email, social media and other options. Then, build a strategy around those channels and continue to test as donors and digital tools evolve.

Email open and response rates for health care solicitation are improving, while at the lower end of the range for charities (environmental groups remain at the top of the range). Direct email asks are coming later to health care than to other charities, in particular when national health care organizations, such as single disease charities, are viewed separately from hospitals and health systems. Email can, however, be a valuable tool for sending updates, electronic impact reports, event invitations or reminders, links to giving day websites and reminders for year-end giving.

Build an email list organically, during regular communication with existing constituents, and integrate email where it is natural. For example, send an email as a lead-up or follow-up to a direct mail letter to increase responses. Use emails from a trusted staff member to communicate with donors in between asks or to show donors how their gifts are used.

Emails can also make giving days, such as Giving Tuesday, more successful by guiding constituents to the landing page. It is important to integrate giving day email content and timing with other regular mail and digital appeals.

Few charitable organizations, including health care organizations, raise significant financial resources directly from social media, such as Facebook. Social media can be a powerful tool, however, for supporting other annual giving programs, such as events, annual honor-a-caregiver appeals or giving day promotions.

For example, when sending direct mail appeals for Doctors' Day, kick off the campaign with postings on Facebook, set up a special landing page for Doctors' Day gifts, feature the opportunity to honor a physician on the organization's web page, send a follow-up email ask to donors with email addresses on file and send a special thank you on Facebook and in email after the campaign is complete. In each case, cross-link between social media and other media.

Online peer-to-peer fundraising, text to give, crowdfunding and other tools can add to annual revenue, while they may or may not help identify and grow relationships with potential major gift donors.

Questions to ask and
answer when planning for
a cross-channel annual
giving strategy include:

• Who are my various donor groups?
• What channels meet their giving
and engagement needs?
• What is right for my patient base
and my community?
• Is an event necessary? What are
the measurable benefits, beyond net
revenue, of investing resources in an
event?
• What age groups and donor profiles
should I target for donor acquisition?
• Am I strategically integrating all
channels in a donor-centered way?

While these can be important tools for grassroots causes and some health care organizations, like children's hospitals, they may not tie easily to pipeline goals.

There are no absolute right or wrong answers, simply what is right for each organization, its resources and core constituency. Today, no one channel provides the silver bullet for revenue and donor development goals. The key to success is to put together a schedule that feels planned and well-coordinated from the donor's point of view while meeting the range of donor needs.

BUILD ENDURING DONOR RELATIONSHIPS BY ACQUIRING AND RETAINING DONORS WITH LONG-TERM VALUE

New donor acquisition is the first step in pipeline development. Acquisition today is extremely competitive, and donors are more fickle than ever. As a result, in the new annual giving paradigm, a donor is tagged as "acquired" only after the second gift, rather than after the first gift. This is a more accurate measure of how many people have chosen to become part of the organization's donor family.

Focus on acquiring donors with the greatest long-term value, the highest likelihood of giving long-term and the capacity to increase giving over time. Likely donors may include patients who want to give back and invest in an organization that has cared for them or may include community members with known interest in supporting health care.

Ask first-time donors to renew in a timely manner, generally within 90 days of the first gift, to secure the highest retention rate.

Make sure they feel fully appreciated for their new support before asking for the second gift. Provide at least one stewardship touch, in addition to an acknowledgment letter. For example, send a "welcome new donor" package or make a personal thank you call.

A key factor to nurturing long-term retention and loyalty is to provide annual donors with seamless and satisfying giving experiences. Baby boomers and younger generations who are beginning to support health care causes seek great experiences throughout their lives, including in their giving lives. Satisfying donor experiences are created through the cumulative effect of personalized acknowledgments, updates on how gifts are used, easy interactions with office staff, accurate names and addresses and any touch that helps them believe they are not being taken for granted as donors.

Allocating time to integrate one-to-one, personal contact with annual donors can also provide multiple benefits. Benefits include:

· improving retention rates
· improving donor satisfaction
· building loyalty, and
· providing hints of interest and readiness to make larger annual or major gifts.

This can take attention and discipline, as annual giving is largely tactical and time intensive by nature.

While loyalty at any gift level is a priority, the development of mid-level and high-value annual donors is a central part of the pipeline development approach to annual giving. The exact value of mid-level and high-value annual donors varies by organization. For some, $1,000 per year is high-value, and for others it is mid-value. Whatever the amount, targeted appeals, special engagement opportunities and increased personal contact can help build loyalty and identify major or planned gift prospects.

Monthly giving is a variation on mid-level donor development. Monthly donors are often a smaller cohort, while they have a higher lifetime value. To develop monthly donors, target recent donors who have already given several gifts. Offer them the option to upgrade to monthly gifts in a specific, targeted ask for the best results.

Overall, the reimagined annual giving program places significant emphasis on pipeline outcomes when choosing channels and designing an integrated annual calendar.

PROVIDE DILIGENT LEADERSHIP FOR ANNUAL GIVING

Adept data management is required to meet today's annual giving donor expectations and to manage the increased complexity of channel integration. Up-to-date software tools are needed to maintain data integrity, segment donor groups, target messages, track donor preferences and measure pipeline development. Sound business processes and well-trained staff are also differentiators.

In time, whole-view CRM (customer relationship management) software will overtake today's more static databases. True CRM tools allow the organization to see all aspects of donor relationships with the organization, manage donor preferences and provide donors the coherent and satisfying relationships they want with their chosen charities.

Data-enabled performance measures also help track progress toward today's pipeline goals. Use traditional measures, such as response rate, average gift, costs of funds raised and return on investment to track individual annual giving channel productivity. Identify a handful of key measures to track pipeline development, such as overall retention rates, number of donors at high-value thresholds and the number of donors identified as major gift prospects. Track the total, long-term value of donors who are nurtured through annual giving and also make major or planned gifts.

Supplement basic annual giving measures with advanced analytics. Track lifetime value of individual donor cohorts, conduct in-depth donor file analyses and use predictive modeling to determine which channels and strategies to emphasize, modify or discontinue.

Questions to ask and answer when evaluating and refining IT capacity:

• How would I rate the integrity of my data? Is it accurate? Clean?

• Am I planning for the future? Investing enough in software capability and staff skill-building?

• Am I using adequate analytics to track progress toward my goals and make sound decisions about my annual giving program?

The modern annual giving leader's role is to embrace the pipeline paradigm, design an integrated plan, be diligent in implementing the plan and advocate for annual giving with other staff and board leadership. It may take time to shift expectations from revenue measures only. If asked, "How much did we raise?", answer by reporting revenue and pipeline development results, such as overall retention rates and the number of donors identified as major gift prospects.

Expect collaboration among development functions to help ensure a seamless donor experience. For example, require direct mail, stewardship and digital team members to coordinate messaging and timing of donor asks and touches.

Break down silos between annual giving and major gifts teams. Create a culture that rewards collaboration, built on the understanding that the donor experience is paramount, and coordination ultimately leads to better results. Design performance incentives so individual team members are rewarded for placing the highest priority on donor needs and interests. For example, recognize when $1,000 high-value annual donors want to remain $1,000 donors. Steward them through the annual giving program, and assign them for major gift cultivation only when it is clear they are ready to move to that stage of the relationship.

Perhaps most importantly, routinely review the profiles of core donor groups. Understand the differences between hospitals, children's hospitals, academic medical centers, hospices and other health care charities. Choose the channels to match and design an annual giving program that relentlessly pursues donor development goals as well as revenue goals.

CHAPTER 7

Advancing a Deeper Approach to Planned Giving

Eddie Thompson, Ed.D., FCEP

As a seasoned philanthropy executive, you understand planned giving, or gift planning, assists donors in making larger gifts than they ever dreamed possible. However, health care philanthropy organizations have developed the habit of seeking gifts from discretionary income and ignoring the enormous potential in gifts from net worth. One of the most valuable lessons a philanthropy organization can learn is that not all donors have the ability to give cash. Because most folks do not consider themselves "wealthy donors," they are nervous about having enough money to live on for the rest of their lives. This causes internal conflict because, while they may have a desire to give, they may not feel they have the means to make those gifts. Thus, planned giving must be an important part of your comprehensive development program, since it provides enormous benefits for the health care organization, including:

- overcoming financial constraints to make a gift that satisfies charitable intent
- creating potential for a much greater contribution than otherwise considered possible
- harnessing a powerful tool to build endowment.

The history of philanthropy is replete with examples of individuals who made an enormous difference because they left an estate gift. Great universities like Harvard, Yale, Princeton, Vanderbilt and Stanford received enormous gifts to build very large endowments. These endowments did not grow overnight. They were years, in fact, decades in the making. They received planned gift after planned gift after planned gift. Their success was measured one planned gift at a time. The history of these organizations is filled with activities, which led to deeper relationships, which concluded with conversations about philanthropy. While these institutions may not have known these gifts were forthcoming, their activities and their conversations with donors ultimately led to these gifts. History reminds us successful fund development requires conversations with individuals who believe in the organizational mission. It is no different if you're seeking a planned gift or a discretionary-income gift. Relationships and stewardship are the two pillars on which successful fund development is built.

If philanthropy organizations want to be successful, it is crucial to keep donors' interests front and center in your approach.

The most successful organizations and planned giving solicitations are donor-centered. It is easy for philanthropy organizations to be centered on themselves. After all, they have budgets and needs which will not be fulfilled without cash. Most philanthropic gift advisors who approach a donor explain in passionate words the mission they seek to achieve. While that is important, donors give based upon their own needs, goals and objectives. If philanthropy organizations want to be successful, it is crucial to keep donors' interests front and center in your approach. This is a lot easier said than done. Budget constraints and other important organizational needs put pressure on philanthropy professionals to think only about the benefit to the health care organization. But, in order to secure a major gift or planned gift, the donor must ask really important questions. However, the more donor-centered you are, the more successful you will be.

Why are some philanthropy organizations more successful in raising money than others? What do they do that makes them stand out above the rest? What are their secrets to success? The best organizations are proactive and strategic, while average organizations are reactive. The average have movement, while the best have momentum. Subtle differences are big differences!

PIECES OF A PLANNED GIVING MOSAIC

The best way to describe planned giving efforts at successful organizations is to see it as a mosaic. Let's assume the four sides of the frame for the mosaic are 1) excellent leadership 2) an appealing mission to change lives 3) a dedicated staff and 4) high visibility among a community of potential donors. These four basic sides of the frame are the essential foundation. However, the frame is not the picture. There are many interlocking pieces to the mosaic of a successful planned giving program. The more pieces of the mosaic a philanthropy organization has in place, the more complete the picture of success becomes.

1) Have more meaningful conversations.

Great conversations imply philanthropic gift advisors listen more than they talk. They have conversations about the health care organization's mission to change lives. Meaningful conversations set the context for planned giving. The request for a planned gift is part of a conversation. It is an important part, but it is still just a part. Successful organizations have more meaningful planning conversations with donors than the average philanthropy organization.

2) Maintain more relationships.

There is a great difference between more relationships and long donor lists. Having someone's name, ID number, address and giving history does not mean you have a relationship with that person. It is more important to have long-term relationships than a long donor list. Great relationships lead to planned gifts, while donor lists lead to average gifts!

3) Make more requests for estate gifts.

Great philanthropic gift advisors ask the donor to join their noble cause and to consider making a financial contribution in a worthwhile effort to change lives. The more people you ask to also make an estate gift, the more money you raise for your mission. In some respects, it is a numbers game but with an important distinction—you ask people with whom you have a real relationship.

4) Observe donors' giving patterns.

Donors have their own giving patterns. They may give at the end of December like many other donors who give in that month. They may give stock from the same company at the same time every year. There's usually a reason for the donor's giving pattern, and it is often methodical. The more you understand the patterns, the more money you will raise.

5) Know why each donor gives and what they are trying to accomplish.

Achieving true understanding is one of your major goals when you are in conversation with supporters. What is their motivation? Why are they investing their resources in your organization? "Why" and "what" are great questions that can lead to amazing discussions. The better you understand the "why" and "what" behind donors' giving decisions, the more planned gifts you will secure.

6) Create meaningful visit reports.

Visit reports are more than just tasks to be completed. They hold great value! They are meaningful and intentional, revealing insights and nuances. These reflections provide guidance for future discussions giving you greater insights to future proposals, which have been shaped by answers to the "why" and "what" questions. Visit reports are similar to mapping territory for the first time. They are like landmarks recorded on a map, allowing you to move to a destination more quickly with less effort. Well-written visit reports are a powerful tool.

7) Thank each donor for every gift and commit to use it wisely.

The best organizations are highly creative in the way they express appreciation. Showing appreciation that gets donors' attention is a real art. Others formalize gift acknowledgment processes to the point it seems sterile and insincere. The promise to use the gift wisely and efficiently is equally important but only as effective as the commitment to follow through on that promise. Together, expressions of appreciation and promises fulfilled set the stage for larger planned gifts.

8) Manage time with done-by-dates.

Done-by-dates lead to greater efficiencies and success. Great organizations have timelines and goals for planned gifts that are clearly established and recorded. They set completion dates and work backward to determine starting times for projects or activities. They break the schedule into small pieces with interim milestones. They reach small goals and dates, which led to great achievements. In other words, they are proactive in their approach and "calendar" their way into securing planned gifts.

9) Use a systematic approach.

Great philanthropic gift advisors know what they are doing and where they are going. There are clear goals and challenges with achievable objectives along the way. Individuals have clearly defined job descriptions which complement other positions within their team. Tasks and responsibilities are understandable and attainable with the proper time allotted for each task. There is no sense of urgency. The team knows their jobs and their roles. There is a system for success in place. They have a plan, and they work the plan.

10) Hold people accountable.

Each person on the team is given a job to do and is expected to do it well. They all understand success together depends on everyone's on-time performance. Executive leadership and administrative staff members are all held accountable for small steps along the way, not just end results — on measurable activities not just results of total dollars raised — but on measurable activities. After all, one could have a great year and have less than great results due to outside influences (e.g. bad economy, death of a major donor, etc.). Achieving successful activities is a better, more fair-minded way of holding one accountable.

11) Communicate with each donor by phone, letter and in person.

Great organizations call donors on the phone, make personal visits, and send non-solicitation letters to share the latest news concerning tax law changes related to philanthropy. They make sure they have more interactions that are educational than just asking for money. You don't want donors to feel that the only time you see them is when you are asking for a gift.

12) Live donor-centered.

Each philanthropy organization is true to their word when it comes to being donor-centered. They place the personal goals and objectives of their supporters ahead of their own interest. This is very difficult to do if your performance is only measured by the amount of money raised.

13) Understand the importance of capacity and constantly evaluate the staging process.

Capacity! Capacity! Capacity! None of the above information matters if you don't have organizational and individual capacity dialed in properly. The average organization staff is overworked, overcommitted and wearing too many hats. They are so busy with unrelated activities that they had little time to have meaningful conversations with a large number of donors. Capacity should be considered on two levels: 1) the number of planned giving prospects who would benefit from meaningful conversations and 2) the number of philanthropic gift advisors you have on staff who understand the opportunities of planned giving. The best organizations have a staff-staging approach based on growth. They intend to raise more money and have a strategic plan to do so. They are proactive rather than reactive with staffing and donor-relations capacity.

14) Balance annual giving, major gifts, planned giving and campaigns.

Resist wanting to have it all and have it all today; have patience. Great leaders understand you can be successful today and tomorrow with a well-planned and balanced approach to annual, major and planning giving alongside successful campaigns. Distribute efforts in a balanced way amongst annual, major, planned giving and campaigns, and simultaneously cultivate in each field. This strategy takes more forethought, strategic efforts and constant evaluation. Understand many donors who are short on cash could contribute from their estates or use of appreciated assets.

15) Ask for gifts of net worth and not just discretionary dollars.

Here's a powerful but simple idea: the largest gifts usually come from a donor's net worth. When you ask for a check (gift from discretionary income), you compete with every other charity, the family vacation or Friday night at the movies. There is so much competition for the discretionary dollar. Every nonprofit organization asks donors to write a check to support their efforts, but the best organizations also ask for gifts of net worth. Harvard University did not build their massive endowment through gifts of discretionary income; they have a long history of asking donors to include them in their estate. Average shops ask for checks. The best philanthropic gift advisors also ask for planned gifts.

16) Have a strategic plan.

Successful organizations always have a strategic plan, a systematic approach and a high level of accountability. The most successful organizations in securing planned gifts employ those same organizational disciplines. In contrast, very few average organizations actually have a strategic fund development plan. Even fewer philanthropy organizations have a strategic plan for planned giving.

OPPORTUNITIES FOR PLANNED GIVING IN HEALTH CARE

Philanthropy in health care is progressing rapidly toward blended gifts, and this is the area with the greatest potential. The concept for blended gifts is very simple. A donor commits to three types of gifts over an extended period of time. They make a large current gift and commit to an annual gift and an estate gift to increase their desired dollar goal for total giving. Donors who have significant charitable intent love this approach. While it is not for every donor, there are a large number of donors who would be open to this approach.

THREE TYPES OF DONORS

There are three types of individuals who make charitable gifts. Deepening your relationship with the donor allows you to determine a donor's type of giving. Philanthropic gift advisors who spend a lot of time talking with donors realize there are certain types who are more likely to make a planned gift. In Harold J. Seymour's book *Design for Fundraising*, he suggests there are three types of donors:

1. The Habitual Donor

The habitual donor gives the same amount of money around the same time of year, each and every year. The challenge with this donor is to get them to increase their annual gift.

2. The Emotional Donor

The emotional donor hears or sees something that leads them to make a gift. These gifts tend to be larger than the habitual donor's gift. The challenge with these donors is the infrequency of gifts. One of the goals for the emotional donor is to get them to give more frequently.

3. The Strategic Donor

The vast majority of philanthropy organizations don't recognize the potential in strategic donors, because they are the not the typical annual or emotional giver. They tend to be a little cranky and unusual. Sometimes their many questions can be a bit unnerving. They tend to be deliberate, cautious and careful accumulators of wealth. They tend to drive cars longer than the average person; they live in smaller houses than they can afford. Consequently, it takes a good deal of time to figure out what motivates their giving decisions. They do not see themselves as simply contributors but as investors, and they are tremendous planned giving prospects. They do make annual gifts; but, because their gifts may be small, many philanthropy organizations never take the time to get to know them—to their peril and great loss. While it takes a great deal of time, effort and energy to get to know them, it is worth the investment.

Why Are Donors so Open to the Concept of a Blended Gift?

• The number of donors who can or will make substantial out-right gifts is very small
• Even donors who have a large estate may not know if they have enough money to live on for the rest of their lives, so they feel unable to make a major gift during their lifetime.

What Are Some of the Motivations for Making a Blended Gift?

Individuals who make this type of gifts are motivated by at least one of these four goals:

• make a difference in the lives of people with needs
• give back to a community that has blessed them
• belong to an effort that is noble
• remember or honor someone they love

AN EXAMPLE OF A BLENDED GIFT:

Jim and Mary Smith (ages 75 and 74) have been strong and frequent supporters of the hospital foundation. They would love to make a substantial gift to the foundation, but they are worried they will not have enough to live on for the rest of their lives. They might be open to a strategy where they could make a gift of a million dollars if they knew how to do it. Jean is a philanthropic gift advisor for the foundation, and she makes the following proposal:

Jim and Mary would be able to memorialize Mary's mother by making a blended gift. Jim and Mary would make a $100,000 IRA rollover gift at the end of the year. They would also make a pledge of $25,000 per year and complete an irrevocable pledge to come from the remainder of their estate to total $1,000,000. This plan allows them to make a large immediate gift, as well as a pledge for the future. Mary's mother has been honored and memorialized. Jim and Mary now feel they have enough to live on for the rest of their lives and are thrilled to know they are making a difference.

THE THREE IMPORTANT QUESTIONS

There are three questions a donor must ask and answer before they give a major gift. It is especially true when you're seeking a planned gift. The three questions are:

1. Do I have enough to live on for the rest of my life?

This is a very difficult question in today's environment. Many donors who wish to give a contribution are simply afraid to give too much, because they don't know what the future holds. There's a greater percent of donors who do not know the answer to this question than those who do. Have you ever known a donor who made a major gift who could not answer this question?

2. What should I do for my heirs?

This is the naughty question. It's the one that is most difficult to answer for many families. It may be they have an evil son-in-law they worry about. It could be they have a special-needs child who requires additional attention. It may be they are worried about a child getting a divorce and becoming financially stranded. There are so many reasons why parents worry about their children. It is important that a donor knows the answer before they make a gift.

3. Would I rather give some of my estate to the IRS or to local charities?

The vast majority of donors would rather give to local charities than leave a portion of their estate to the Internal Revenue Service. It may be we are so busy trying to raise discretionary income gifts that we fail to seek gifts of net worth, which flow from an estate plan. Educating donors about these potential gifts may answer questions that give them pause and prevent them from making a decision about gifts from their estate. The more you educate donors on the potential of making these gifts, the more of these gifts will flow into your organization.

It is important to not rush donors when it comes to securing a planned gift. They need time to think about this important decision. Most donors do not need advice on what they *should* do; they simply need more information on what they *can* do.

STRATEGIC DONORS MOST FREQUENTLY MAKE BLENDED GIFTS

Strategic donors are instrumental accumulators of wealth. They are often overlooked by philanthropy professionals. They have high donor intent, but often make "small" gifts. They glow with pride about your organization and have built their wealth in unrealized income. They are highly motivated to give back.

Where Do You Start?

The starting point is to make sure your gift acceptance policies address the type of gifts used to create a blended gift. It is important to establish standards for accounting and counting a blended gift. It would be valuable to have a strategy meeting with the development team to create a prospect list of potential donors for these types of gifts. The next step would be to prepare a number of blended gift arrangements along with supporting documents to educate and motivate donors. Spread the good news of the potential benefits of blended gifts in every mailing to donors.

YOUR BEST PROSPECTS

The most logical starting point for a planned giving program is with those closest to the organization; they are most likely to lead in making planned gifts. Start with staff, board and top donors. Certain types of individuals or couples are your best prospects. They are:

Single Individuals without Children

These individuals are excellent planned giving prospects. It is important to remember they tend to be cautious accumulators of wealth. They will tell you they have no one to depend upon but themselves. So, they tend to save more and live more modestly than the average person. These single adults without children are among your greatest planned giving prospects.

INFRASTRUCTURE FOR PLANNED GIVING

COMPUTER SOFTWARE
Utilize software specifically designed to run planned giving calculations and to create gift illustrations for prospective donors. But remember—even a well-defined proposal cannot replace a meaningful personal visit with a donor.

MARKETING
Establish a strategic marketing plan and continue to follow the plan even if you don't see immediate results. There are a number of companies that can help deliver valuable information to your donors and do so with high standards.

HERITAGE SOCIETIES
One of the best ways to steward a planned-gift donor is to invite them into your organization's "heritage society." There are a couple reasons why this is a good investment of your time. It allows you to show appreciation to those who've made a statement or planned gifts to your organization in a group setting. It also reinforces to the donor that they're involved with other individuals in a noble cause.

WORKING WITH PROFESSIONAL ADVISORS
Take time to explain the mission and purpose of your organization to professional advisors. While it is not their job to secure gifts for your organization, they may be able to help in the right circumstance. Invite them to tour your campus to see the good that you are doing.

BUDGETING FOR SUCCESS
We have all heard the statement, "It takes money to make money." However, it is amazing how many philanthropy organizations want a strong planned giving program but are unwilling to invest. There needs to be a line item in the budget to fund a solid planned giving program, including allowances for travel, entertainment, marketing and training.

Couples without Children

These couples are excellent prospects for the very same reason described of the single individual. In some cases, couples choose not to have children. More often, it wasn't because they didn't try.

In either case, couples without children may be even more acutely aware of the legacy issue. They want to be remembered by future generations as people who left the world a better place. These are great prospects that should not be overlooked.

Couples with Successful Children

These couples frequently do not feel the need to leave a large inheritance to their children because their children have been so successful. It is important to let donors define what it means to be "successful." You'll often hear them say, "You would not believe how much my son or daughter makes." You might also hear them say, "You would not believe how large my child's house is." Both these donors are frequently volunteers for your organization. Their personal contact with those in your organization increases their potential for planned giving.

Individuals with Successful Children

These donors are also excellent prospects for the very same reason couples with successful children are. One additional factor, there is one less question individuals have to answer: couples do not know who will outlive the other. Consequently, there is an added level of caution. However, single individuals without dependents are more at ease making very generous planned gifts.

Parents Afraid of Leaving Their Children a Large Inheritance

There may be several reasons why parents hesitate to leave their children a large inheritance. It may be one of their children is a special needs child. It may be they have a child or grand-child with an addiction, and leaving them a large inheritance could only lead to greater destruction. There are many reasons why some parents are nervous about leaving a large inheritance. They may be open, however, to leaving their children a stream of income, which might be satisfied by using a testamentary charitable remainder trust.

THREE TYPES OF PLANNED GIFTS

The three basic types of planned gifts are:

1. Bequests
There are four types of bequests.

a. Specific Bequest: This is where a donor leaves a specific item to a philanthropy organization.

b. Percentage Bequest: This is where a donor leaves a percent of their estate or residuary to a charity.

c. Residuary Bequest: This is where a donor leaves whatever's left after making a specific bequest to other heirs or to charity.

d. Then, there is the bequest that states if everybody in my family has passed away – along with all of my friends, acquaintances and pets then, whatever's left goes to charity. This, by the way, is the most frequent bequest.

2. Gifts from Contractual Arrangements
These gifts are the result of a donor designating the organization as the beneficiary of a retirement account, insurance, investments, irrevocable pledge or bequest, etc. These gifts are frequently overlooked, but there is enormous potential in asking your donors to include your organization on their beneficiary forms.

3. Split Interest Gifts
These gifts provide an income to the donor or a designated person. This type of gifts include:

a. Charitable gift annuities (CGA);

b. Charitable remainder trust (CRT);

c. Charitable lead trust (CLT); and,

d. Remainder life estate.

Parents Who Do Not Feel the Need to Leave Their Children a Large Inheritance

You probably know a number of families where philanthropy is a generational trait. You probably have a number of your donors who believe their children are incredibly successful and do not feel the need to leave them a large inheritance. They are probably already current major gift donors. While these donors are few in number, the potential for planned gifts is staggering.

Donors Who Have Built Up Unrealized Gain

These donors are often business folks. They may have purchased a piece of property outside of town twenty-five years ago, and now it's worth an incredible amount of money. It may be that they started a very small business in their home twenty-five or thirty years ago, and it has become a radically appreciated asset. Now, they're ready to sell. Individuals who have unrealized gain, or capital gains, are excellent prospects for the obvious reasons.

Blended Families

This group is made up primarily of senior citizens who have lost their spouse and have now remarried. They have some peculiar needs that may be addressed by using charitable arrangements. They may share a home but often have separate checking accounts, cars and investments. There are planned gift arrangements that may specifically address some of the needs this group encounters. Again, it's a small group with a great deal of potential.

It is very important that when helping a donor decide what giving arrangement is best for them you allow their advisors to provide counsel. Never overstep the boundary by trying to provide legal or tax advice. Allow their advisors to lead the process.

Working with donors in the profession of planned giving is very exciting. Dream big dreams about the difference your efforts will have on your organization's very important mission. You will love the conversations you have with donors that lead to oganization-changing gifts. Now, roll up your sleeves as you head out of your office to change your life and those you serve.

Now, the fun begins!

CHAPTER 8

Driving Strategically Aligned Project Selection

Betsy Chapin Taylor, FAHP

Health care is in a period of disruptive change. Faced with soaring technology and drug costs, introduction of new treatment modalities, need for infrastructure and programs to support population health and pressure to constantly improve quality and patient safety, hospital budgets are stressed as never before. Enormous investments in information technology are needed to support new clinical and operational systems. And, while health systems must stay competitive and keep their populations healthy by charging full speed ahead to finance and build community-based physician offices, ambulatory care clinics and other outpatient facilities, aging inpatient infrastructures groan under the need for modernization, renovation and replacement.

The stress of meeting all these critically important needs - especially during a period of massively changing reimbursement mechanisms and uncertain government funding - is taking its toll. The days of belt-tightening and cost reduction efforts to make ends meet are over. These challenges are driving the need for alternative revenue resources, as financial capacity has become a primary limiting factor on organizational progress. The availability of capital for key projects is shrinking, and many organizations have delayed or canceled major investments due to market forces. To move forward, the industry is in desperate need of a financial "game changer."

As more and more leading health systems are finding, one of the game changers can be...philanthropy. Health care philanthropy can evolve into a powerhouse that nurtures and develops reliable funding streams to support the health system's vision and top strategic priorities. Yet, many organizations squander the potential impact of philanthropy by allowing charitable dollars to benefit low value activities and initiatives.

To harness philanthropy's potential, health care organizations must tightly align philanthropic funding opportunities with the health care organization's strategic priorities and aspirations to maximize impact. While facilitating a process to improve project selection requires diligence and coordination across the organization, achieving integration and alignment is an ambition worth pursuing that will reposition a key stream of revenue from "value added" to high impact and will inspire donors to give more as they have confidence gifts are being utilized for the highest and best use.

RECAPTURING OPPORTUNITY

Health care organizations have become increasingly diligent and strategic about their financial and capital planning efforts. The abundance of delayed investments and new aspirations for investment clearly outstrip resources, and scarcity means every dollar must be squeezed to fulfill the mission and to capture competitive advantage. This reality compels health care organizations to create more robust decision-making processes and to enlarge the number of stakeholders around the table to allocate capital and other resources.

Despite heightening diligence around the allocation of other organizational financial resources, there is often little attention paid to using charitable dollars strategically. This lost opportunity likely stems from the fact that many health care organizations have traditionally used philanthropy for value-added initiatives that are "nice to have" rather than core initiatives that are "essential to have." The problem often begins in innocuous ways:

· The foundation board or its allocations committee perceives philanthropy is intended to be a value-add, and the group has discretion to surface and select projects outside current capital and operating budgets and strategic priorities. This not only fuels funding efforts that are often tangential to priorities but also means the foundation is de facto setting strategy for the health care organization. This is further exacerbated by the fact that decisions are often made without the insights and expertise of health care executives and physicians who have a finger on the pulse of a changing health care industry, shifting demographics, the competitive landscape or more. Further, the philanthropy organization exists solely to strengthen and sustain the health care organization's mission, so funding priorities should support the health care organization's assessment of how it can best fulfill its mission. While this poor, historical allocation practice is starting to wane, it is time to stamp it out —both donors and boards have a vested interest in maximizing the impact of philanthropic dollars on the mission.

· Health care executives and the governing board see philanthropy as a resource to take care of "all the other things" after the hospital has taken care of "all the things that are important." This occurs as leaders choose for the health care organization to use its capital budget or resources to fund the organization's most important and most strategic projects. Then, projects that fall lower on the prioritization list for investment are turned over to the philanthropy organization to seek charitable dollars for funding. However, having the health care organization sweep up all transformational projects with strategic consequences and significant donor appeal dampens the case for significant philanthropy and puts the foundation in the position of trying to galvanize interest in a project that does not have emotional appeal or that will not materially change patient outcomes or meaningfully raise the standard of care. As a consequence, the foundation is left with all the leftover lemons that were abandoned on the chopping block. Now, the philanthropy organization pushes hard on a case with little resonance and raises an amount of money that undercuts the true potential for community charitable giving. Offloading projects the health care organization has no strong interest in funding to the philanthropy organization not only undervalues and poorly utilizes community giving but also decreases the incentive for executive, board and physician engagement in advancing philanthropy.

The prevalent practice of health care organizations funding what they perceive as important while leaving leftovers to philanthropy fails to recognize something simple and obvious: All organizational dollars are effectively in a closed system. The health care organization and its affiliated philanthropy organization both intend to deploy their financial assets toward the advancement of the health care mission, so both health care organization dollars and philanthropic dollars should be viewed as "sources" to fund the various "uses" in the organization. Therefore, the health care organization should be indifferent what the foundation funds as long as it is on the strategic priority list. If the foundation can generate more donor interest and excitement raising money for

Strategy and philanthropy are integrally connected disciplines when executed well.

the organization's top priority to drive innovation in cancer care than they can for a priority that didn't "make the list" to replace equipment in the physical therapy gym, then the foundation should fund the cancer project and allow the health care organization to redirect its dollars to PT. Basically, when donors respond to a call to action for a significant project, the health care organization can redirect funds to projects with less donor appeal that are further down their own list. When this occurs, the organization simultaneously enhances total dollars raised and frees money to invest in other organizational priorities....so everyone wins.

Strategy and philanthropy are integrally connected disciplines when executed well. Without alignment, fund development is an arbitrary endeavor that is indifferent to enabling high value or low value activities. Failure to select projects well also presents a breakdown in the value chain for health care philanthropy organizations. Organizations that cannot identify projects and articulate their value well have a hollow case that can be a severe limiting factor on attracting significant investment. However, with alignment, the organization can enunciate a clear and compelling vision of what the organization could be if it achieved its potential. Strategically aligned project selection leads to having an urgent, compelling and potentially transformational case for support that can foster outsize donor interest and investment.

DONORS EXPECT MORE

Enhancing project selection not only increases organizational impact but also elevates what a donor is able to achieve. Significant donors want to invest in high impact, high priority projects to advance the health care organization's strategic vision and core mission.

Donors today are discriminating. They seek clear and specific impact demonstrated by measurable outcomes that are directly attributable to charitable investments. Donor investors share "giving to a program, project, or area of focus that is specific and measurable is essential." [1] "Savvy donors increasingly invest in high performers, while dropping low performers and institutions unable to validate worth with gift impact data."[2] The drive for impact also means donors often restrict the use of their gifts to particular initiatives rather than giving unrestricted gifts, so it behooves the organization to articulate where investment would matter most. Simply, donors rightly expect a meaningful return on their charitable investment.

Significant donors generally do not rise to the bait of "need." Health care reimbursements declining or changing are not a compelling reason to invest. That's because significant donors seek organizations that propose to utilize their expertise and unique understanding to enable and expand valuable solutions rather than back-filling budgets. Donors respond to well-managed organizations with abundant opportunities to pursue rather than abundant needs to share. Further, 89 percent of affluent donors indicate it is important for an organization "demonstrate sound business and operational practices" for them to have confidence to invest. [3] Simply, charitable investors respond to financial stability, organizational sustainability...and big ideas.

Donors seek collective and collaborative solutions. There is keen recognition that many health care and societal problems cannot be wholly addressed by a single provider or solution. In fact, health care donors "are becoming more interested in funding collaborative initiatives to drive systemic change." [4] This preference and inclination aligns well with health care's new ambition to fund community impact projects under the umbrella of population health. It also means organizations must pivot from an orientation based in articulating a rationale for giving that rallies exclusively around their brand and legacy to share an expansive vision for change.

Philanthropy remains an avenue for individuals to fulfill their deeper purpose. Donors remain motivated by values, meaning and an opportunity to have an impact on the world. In fact, almost half of affluent individuals express seeing charitable giving as a way to have the "greatest potential for positive impact on society." [5] This means that, again, sharing a vision that is incremental or uninspiring doesn't cut it. Purpose, meaning and self-actualization are rarely fulfilled by investing in something that slipped off the bottom of the health care organization's list of priorities.

All of these motivations—from a desire for impact to a desire to enable solutions to a desire to fulfill one's individual purpose—make it incumbent on the health care organization to invite donors to be part of significant work. Organizations owe donor partners who aim to stand shoulder to shoulder with the organization to transform health care the courtesy of sharing the organization's most compelling and most impactful vision of potential.

BUILDING A BETTER FRAMEWORK

Making a switch to high impact, aligned philanthropy requires both diligent process and inclusion of the right people with the right information and the right sets of decision rights to make solid and binding decisions. This means the chief philanthropy officer no longer sits in her office alone digging through a pile of spreadsheets trying to identify projects with potential philanthropic merit; she collaborates with key organizational allies to craft an approach to optimize the opportunity for philanthropic investment. Now, project selection becomes a deliberate organizational endeavor advanced with collaboration between health care executives, governing board trustees, foundation board members and often physicians or other allies.

There is a dual intention in undergoing a strategically aligned project selection process like this. The organization not only is selecting priorities but also is enabling a pivot in how philanthropic funds are deployed. Instead of the philanthropy organization securing and collecting charitable contributions across the course of a year to then distribute after-the-fact through allocations, the organization selects specific initiatives and focus areas for which philanthropy professionals will proactively seek charitable investments. This gives donors clear and specific priorities in which to

127

prospectively consider investment, and the philanthropy organization has a vibrant case for support. Given that significant donors are inclined to restrict gifts to specific purposes, it also means temporarily restricted contributions are directed toward funds the health care organization would anticipate using in the short or mid-term.

The selection process begins with health care organization executives, since these leaders have the most comprehensive information and understanding about how the organization plans to respond to emerging clinical care needs or shifting demographics and how potential projects fit into the context of what is going on in the health care sector. To kickoff the selection process, organizational leadership must identify those select priorities that will enable the health care organization to advance its strategy. The first stop is considering efforts outlined in the organizational strategic plan. Leaders also harvest prospective ideas from a variety of other documents, to include:

- capital budget planning
- community needs assessment
- master facility plan
- business development plans
- operational budget planning processes
- long-term financial planning documents

In some organizations, executives like to go beyond existing internal plans and documents to effectively issue an internal request for proposals to key organizational and clinical leaders. This offers a variety of positive benefits, including creating broader ownership of the process, ensuring everyone felt they had a voice and uncovering innovative ideas that might not have yet percolated into more formal plans. However, broad inclusion can also bring politics to the table as organizational and clinical leaders often lobby for advancement of their own ideas, and it can surface tangential ideas that have not been vetted at the same level as priorities already included in organizational plans. If the organization pursues this route, the request for proposal generally seeks information on the proposed project, the population it would serve, the anticipated impact, how impact would be measured, cost, timeline and the names of clinical champions who would be advocates in sharing the philanthropic case for support with prospective donors.

As executives consider various potential projects, it is worth the chief philanthropy officer reminding the group that donors generally seek high impact projects that directly enhance the physical, social, emotional or spiritual well-being of patients, families and the community at large. It's also imperative to ensure the ambition extends beyond capital. Leaders often default to identifying facility additions and upgrades or technology and equipment needs. However, sophisticated, impact-driven donors can embrace a broader scope of priorities to include initiatives around innovation, patient safety, quality, patient experience and more. Donors also get excited about ambitions that flow from the transition

It's also imperative to ensure the ambition extends beyond capital.

to values-based care such as community health, community partnerships, prevention, wellness and efforts to address social determinants of health. So, as the organization considers possibilities, it's wise to look at all elements driving transformation. Sample project categories include:

- community partnerships and initiatives that enable the organization to address complex health issues and social determinants of health, i.e. population health
- building to expand capacity, enable advanced care or enhance environment
- clinical programs that add capability or fill existing or emerging needs
- technology that enables new clinical capabilities and better outcomes

· efforts to enhance social, emotional and spiritual support of patients
· outreach and prevention initiatives to enhance community wellness
· innovation of various types to improve quality or safety
· research to advance discovery and capability
· academic and clinical education to prepare high caliber practitioners

Once an initial list of projects has been created, there is value to facilitating a collaborative discussion forum to pressure test items on the list. This forum would typically include a hand-selected group of leaders from various perspectives: health care executives, key clinical service line leaders, governing board trustees, foundation board members and clinicians. This group expands the number of constituencies and perspectives not only to deepen the collective wisdom of the group but also to foster ownership by including key constituencies whose endorsement will be essential moving forward. For example, health care governing board members –particularly those from finance or strategic planning committees– bring not only in-depth knowledge of the organization's strategic and financial plans but also valuable external perspectives and expertise from their own professional endeavors. Foundation board members bring the perspective of sensitivity to donor interests, breadth and depth of the existing donor base and availability of volunteer advocates who could assist in making connections. Physicians and clinicians bring a unique understanding of the clinical merits of various endeavors and deep insight into grateful patients and family members who may have an interest in championing a project. Broad composition around this table is important, since it cures a potential asymmetry of information to improve decision-making and sets a standard of collaboration and alignment between the health care organization, its key organizational allies and its philanthropic arm.

Once assembled, this group is charged to objectively vet projects against a range of filters to determine their fitness to be philanthropic funding priorities. The first set of filters is around the donor appeal of the project. Simply, if it is not something donors would care about it, it does not matter how sound the business case is for it. The chief philanthropy officer is essential in evaluating the donor appeal of a project and in identifying known donors with linkage to the project. Questions to consider include:

· Would this dramatically ENHANCE outcomes or standard of care?
· Is the project RELATABLE and understandable to the public?
· Would this project create EXCITEMENT to ignite donor enthusiasm?
· Would this project make a positive IMPACT on a significant number of people?
· Will the proposed OUTCOMES be clear and measurable?
· Is there an emotional patient STORY to illustrate the importance?
· Is there a PHYSICIAN CHAMPION to actively explain the clinical benefits?
· Is the project UNIQUE relative to real or perceived competitors?

THE LEVER OF THE WHITE COAT

As the organization selects a slate of appropriate projects for philanthropy, it's important to factor in the availability of a committed physician champion. Physician partners are uniquely qualified to enunciate the clinical impact of a project and to add credibility to the effort. Multiple studies show physicians also have the strongest influence on a prospective donor's decision to participate.

Confronting each of these issues starts to illuminate which projects should move forward for additional consideration—or not. Simply, not all strategic projects are suitable for charitable support: some aren't relatable or meaningful for donors and will not gain meaningful traction, so these initiatives should be eliminated from the list.

Projects that do advance should receive additional consideration around elements of business diligence. Issues to explore include:

· Is the project financially SUSTAINABLE once fully operational?

· Does the TIMELINE for acquisition or start allow adequate time to campaign?

· Is the AMOUNT achievable and meaningful?

· Does the project meet BUSINESS DILIGENCE standards go forward?

· Does the organization have the CREDIBILITY to advance the initiative?

· Is there confidence the initiative will gain CON or other APPROVALS to advance?

· Does the organization have RELATIONSHIPS with or access to those with likely affinity and ability to give at an investment level?

THE SENSITIVITY OF TIMING

Many organizations find their financial planning horizons are focused toward investments in the following fiscal year. However, there needs to be adequate time to identify, educate, engage and solicit donors when projects are slated for philanthropic investment. Many organizations break a trust with donors by saying "we need your help" to advance an initiative. Then, the organization proceeds with the project before donor investment has been secured. For that reason, it is advisable to have a window between project selection and project execution consistent with the number and size of gifts that must be secured.

PUTTING KEY QUESTIONS IN ACTION

You can improve the power of the alignment process through effective facilitation of the group. Utilizing the grid on page 134 can be helpful in injecting objectivity in the process and in providing numerical scores to use in ranking. To use the grid, place the names of all proposed projects on the left side of a grid with all criteria across the top; then, award 2 points for "yes", 1 point for "maybe" and 0 points for "no". Add up points for each project after going through the filters for donor appeal to see what stands out, since strength in the "donor appeal" category is critical to proceed even if functional requirements are solid. It is recommended that no project that scores less than a 12 move on to consideration of the business diligence aspects. It should be noted that there are almost always people in the room who will vigorously advocate for their preferred projects, so the facilitator must be able to stay above the politics and personalities to objectively move the process forward

Once the group has considered both sets of questions, every project left on the list is both strategic and will meaningfully fulfill the organization's charitable purpose. The list has also typically been narrowed to a handful of strategic opportunities that have clearly risen to the top. Now, the group can decide if it must utilize discretion to narrow the list further based on the relative strategic merit of the projects, availability of interested donors, timeline for execution or other factors. Then, it is recommended the final list go before the foundation board of directors for their consideration and input, since leadership volunteers who will be advancing the identification, cultivation and solicitation of prospective donor partners must have input and ownership of the funding priorities to be presented. The foundation board is also uniquely qualified to consider which opportunities will resonate with existing and prospective donor partners and where there is affinity and alignment between projects, existing physician champions, organizational advocates and existing and prospective donor partners.

FIGURE 8.1

PROJECT	Implement EMR	Advance Clinical Innovation Initiative	Fund Care for the Less Fortunate	Replace Gurneys in ER	Build New Burn Unit	Expand Oncology Services	
Enhance	2	2	0	0	2	2	DONOR APPEAL REQUIREMENTS
Relatable	0	2	1	1	0	2	
Excitement	0	2	0	0	0	2	
Impact	2	2	2	2	0	2	
Unique	0	2	0	0	2	1	
Story	0	2	1	0	1	2	
Champion	0	2	0	0	1	2	
Outcomes	2	2	1	1	2	2	
DONOR APPEAL TOTAL	6	16	5	4	8	15	
Sustainable	2	1	0	2	0	2	FUNCTIONAL REQUIREMENTS
Timeline	1	2	2	2	2	1	
Amount	1	1	1	2	1	1	
Diligence	2	2	1	2	0	2	
FUNCTIONAL TOTAL	6	6	4	8	3	6	

This clean, simple, deliberate and inclusive process effectively uncovers synergy between the health care organization's strategic priorities and opportunities for philanthropic investment to maximize the impact of donor dollars. The process agilely balances competing needs and values and mitigates internal politics and power struggles. The process also enables organizations to make the pivot from reactive allocations to proactive fund development and to overcome philanthropy being an afterthought. It also hardwires vision as the key ingredient in creating an urgent and compelling case for support. Finally, the process is generally easy to integrate into an annual workflow for on-going evaluation of strategic opportunities.

CONCLUSION

Agile and effective decision-making around organizational priorities and deployment of resources is a critical competency for the long-term success of a health care organization. While undergoing a proactive, process-driven approach to enable project selection requires diligence, coordination and collaboration across the organization, achieving integration and alignment optimizes project selection for both annual and campaign efforts and better meets the expressed expectations of thoughtful donor investors. Ultimately, achieving strategic alignment between the health care organization's strategic priorities and philanthropic funding priorities harnesses the considerable power of philanthropy.

References

1. Cygnus Applied Research, Inc.: "The Burk Donor Study: Where Philanthropy is Headed in 2017." http://cygresearch.com/shop-the-burk-donor-survey-2017/. 11.

2. Advisory Board: "Fulfilling the Donor Investor Mandate." https://www.advisory.com/research/philanthropy-leadership-council/studies/2014/fulfilling-the-donor-investor-mandate. 7.

3. Bank of America: "2016 U.S. Trust Study of High Net Worth Philanthropy Reveals Positive Giving and Volunteering Forecasts for the Coming Years." http://newsroom.bankofamerica.com/press-releases/global-wealth-and-investment-management/2016-us-trust-study-high-net-worth-philanthro.

4. "Giving USA 2017," Giving USA, https://givingusa.org/tag/giving-usa-2017/. 253.

CHAPTER 9
Advancing Population Health

Amy Dorrill, FAHP, CRFE

It is essential for health care philanthropy leaders to understand population health and what caused the shift from a fee-for-service to a fee-for-value population-based reimbursement structure to effectively share the rationale for supporting population health through philanthropy.

The traditional health care delivery model has not been working. The United States spends more on health care than any other high-income nation—at a cost of $9,237 per person. Despite the United States' costly investment in health care, the U.S. sees poorer results on key health indicators, such as life expectancy and the prevalence of chronic diseases. National healthcare expenditure projections for 2016-2025 show U.S. health care spending accounts for 18% of the gross domestic product, and it is expected to grow to nearly 20% by 2025. The population aged 65 and over, which represents the heaviest users of health care, is projected to increase to account for more than 20% of the total population by 2050. Aging populations and increased longevity, coupled with chronic health problems, have become a global challenge, putting expanded demands on medical and social services. To try to solve the country's health disparities, health care is making a transformational shift from an acute care delivery model to an integrated care approach focused on population health.

The term "population health" was formally introduced in 2003 by David Kindig and Greg Stoddart to refer to "the health outcome of a group of individuals, including the distribution of such outcomes within the group." Today, the concept of population health is still without a clear, uniform definition. The broad definition aims to improve the health of an entire human population, which leaves plenty of room for differences in interpretation. The term "population" is defined as a particular group of people, such as all patients with a certain disease, or the term can describe all patients living within a geographic area or having a particular type of health insurance. Definitions have varied with some targeting outcomes of population health while others have focused on measurements or accountability. While a standard definition is not yet universally used, the intent is to improve health care outcomes for a population by bringing together a multitude of community organizations and resources.

Population health strives to involve the patient in his own health care by providing more information...

Population health is patient centered. It aligns with the Institute for Healthcare Improvement's Triple Aim to improve patient experience, improve the health of populations and reduce the cost of care. Population health strives to involve the patient in his own health care by providing more information on condition, educating patients on healthy opportunities and modifiable behavior changes that can enhance and maintain wellness and engaging a patient in decisions for his individualized care plan.

Population health expects to reduce overall health care expenses by reducing readmissions, emergency room visits and expensive procedures by shifting the focus from the historical acute care model, which is performed primarily within a hospital or other health care organization, to moving the majority of care and resources outside hospital walls to focus on preventative measures. Key strategies for population health include: increasing the number of covered lives, care coordination, joint partnerships and increased presence within the community focusing on specific demographics or health conditions. The shift will cause hospitals to look beyond pure medical care and will involve a public health perspective encompassing health literacy, education, jobs, smoking, transportation, access to healthy foods and parks and more.

THE CASE FOR PHILANTHROPY

Achieving the aforementioned targets will require a change in the way health care providers are incentivized and reimbursed. Health care payers are shifting from a fee-for-service model based on a volume approach to a fee-for-value model based on the value and results of the intervention and treatment. Value-based reimbursement incentivizes providers to deliver a higher quality of care at the lowest cost to ultimately benefit the provider, the payer and the patient. Hospitals are beginning to see a transition in fee structures and a shift in incentives and penalties. Currently, Medicare has established a continuum of alternative payment structure ranging from small fees and payments based on quality measures and penalties for unacceptable results. For example, hospitals now face a penalty for thirty-day readmissions. And, the continuum will advance to a model that provides complete ownership to providers to take care of a specific population. While some incentives do exist, hospitals are not currently reimbursed for the majority of the organizational and community initiatives required to shift from volume-based to the value-based population health approach.

139

While more than 90% of hospitals agree or strongly agree population health is aligned with their mission, only 19% of health care leaders strongly agree they possess the financial resources needed to support population health. Lack of financial resources and uncertainty about concrete incentive programs are significant barriers for health care organizations to engage in community health improvements. The reality is, most health care systems and hospitals will look at the philanthropy organization to provide financial and other resources to initiate and sustain these initiatives. Understanding population health, hospital plans and expected outcomes is essential for philanthropy leaders to illuminate the opportunity in the face of inherent uncertainty and complexity and to effectively partner with health care executives and to educate and inspire donors.

The philanthropy organization has a multitude of opportunities to support population health, including funding the start-up of new models of care and supporting the structure until the population is large enough or efficient enough to make efforts cost neutral or profitable. A survey of 300 health care executives, administered by the consulting firm KPMG, agreed it would take less than four years to see a positive return on investment, but more than 40% stated the initial cost was a barrier that would make philanthropy essential. Private philanthropy can also fund patient-valued elements of the health care experience similar to the current fund development model and expand to more audacious, holistic initiatives involving internal and external community partnerships.

PHILANTHROPY MUST BE PRESENT AND VOCAL

To be most successful, philanthropy professionals must be present for leadership discussions during the initiation and planning of population health strategies. Similar to the current capital needs approach where capital projects best suited for philanthropic support are identified, the philanthropy office needs to help identify which initiatives and projects within the scope of population health align with private support. This not only involves identifying what is fundable from each selected project but also designing how to communicate to the public and to individual donors and prospects. In selecting projects suited for private support, the following questions should be addressed:

- · how will the project impact patients and the community?
- · what is unique about this project?
- · why is this project or initiative needed?
- · why is this institution best positioned to lead this initiative?
- · what value does philanthropy provide to the project?
- · is the project sustainable?

As always, development must ensure philanthropic funding priorities align with donor interest instead of filling a financial gap of line items not reimbursed by insurers. For example, while it might be difficult to seek funding for the difference in the cost versus reimbursement for a patient visit within a medical home, it is reasonable to assume private funding can be secured to convene a support group, add home visits or telehealth or even to add a handy man service to ensure the home is able to support the patient's needs within a medical home model. These programs could be enticing either to a donor who has benefited from a similar program and has experienced the impact or to a donor who experienced a lack of access to such a program.

DONOR COMMUNICATION

Donor education is key in supporting value-based population health. At the least, understanding population health philanthropy does require a reframing of fund development strategy and donor communication. Effectively communicating the case is imperative for donors to understand the connection and importance of influencing modifiable health risk behaviors to prevent chronic illness and to reduce suffering and early death. To inspire population health donors, philanthropic gift advisors must develop a deep grasp of the strategies and complex issues along with the anticipated outcomes that are not only directly influenced by the hospital but also reflect a global, community-wide perspective. The focus of fund development shifts from the health care organization or system's organizational priorities and projects to a more complex, comprehensive, community-wide approach. For example, talking to a donor interested in diabetes care at the hospital could expand to conversations about not only the value of access to diabetes education, early diagnosis and physician expertise provided within a traditional hospital to manage diabetes but also the conversation may encompass coordination of care for the patient after discharge and external factors shown to reduce the onset of diabetes including building accessible trails and parks, providing education and facilitating access to healthy foods for high risk populations. Whether focusing on capital equipment or care coordination, a key strategy for population health, the attraction to a donor remains the impact on the patient. Just as a philanthropic case for support does not concentrate on the equipment as much as on what the equipment will do, the same is true with packaging the value of a nurse navigator providing care coordination-- the focus is on how the nurse navigator can make a difference in the patient's care. Philanthropy professionals will need to communicate the value proposition and translate abstract, elusive priorities to make them concrete for the donor. To educate the community, it is essential to partner with hospital marketing to communicate a cohesive, overall impact for care coordination and other population health initiatives as well as inspiring personal success stories.

The focus of fund development shifts from the health care organization or system's organizational priorities and projects to a more complex, comprehensive, community-wide approach.

MORE THAN FINANCIAL INVESTMENT

In addition to facilitating philanthropic support, philanthropy professionals can also serve another purpose. In most health care organizations, the philanthropy office is a key community bridge to organizations including other nonprofits and can assist with developing and deepening community relationships and with facilitating hospital leadership identifying the best organizations for collaboration.

COMMUNITY PARTNERS

Population health dictates the patient care model will shift from a silo approach to a more comprehensive network model to enhance care coordination. Hospital systems have historically reacted to address the acute care needs of patients once problems present themselves while the factors contributing to the root cause have been out of the scope of the health care system. For example, the Institute of Medicine (IOM) released a report in 2013 showing one third of adults in the United States were obese in 2012— which is fifteen percent higher than any other country. Obesity alone is associated with higher risk of more than twenty chronic diseases causing a prevalence of health issues, increased mortality and high health care costs. Other potential contributors to the United States' low health outcomes are the large population of uninsured, the environment, lifestyles and rates of accidents and violence which are also out of the scope of traditional health care system strategies. Focus must move from a reactive approach to one that incorporates preventative and sustained behavioral changes.

Eighty percent of what affects health outcomes is associated with factors outside the traditional boundaries of a hospital including health behaviors (tobacco use, sexual activity), social and economic factors (employment, education, income) and physical environment (air quality, water quality). Incentives within Accountable Care Organizations (ACOs) and value-based, risk sharing population contracts encourage hospitals to expand their reach into the community

143

to improve non-medical factors by creating community programs to improve such things as access to housing, availability of healthy food and improved education. Required community health needs assessments identify existing health care resources and prioritize community health needs within the nonprofit hospital's community to not only include charity care and unreimbursed patient care but also activities that affect social determinants of health. In order to make these types of changes, it will take the engagement of numerous organizations from a multitude of sectors.

Organizations with leadership committed to tackling core determinants of health have been early movers in building community-based programs and partnerships. While these initiatives are non-reimbursable, early adopters believe the effort will create overall cost savings to the organization in a value-based fee structure, and these leaders believe community investments address their nonprofit mission. Examples of partnerships include:

- increasing physical activity by developing trails and parks with community or governmental partners
- increasing healthy diets by designing neighborhood gardens, implementing healthy options in schools and providing access to quality food at affordable prices in local grocery stores
- reducing homelessness by partnering with banks and community housing organizations to provide affordable housing
- establishing non-smoking policies for businesses and public areas

Small hospitals are at a greater disadvantage in building and implementing such efforts, because many don't have reserves or resources for capital dollars to develop a new model of care. In comparison, many academic health centers have a natural advantage to utilize internal resources from schools of public health, nursing, medicine and business to develop innovative care models and to serve as a catalyst for inviting other nonprofit and for-profit organizations to collaborate.

HEALTH CARE & PHILANTHROPIC PARTNERSHIPS

Hospitals and other nonprofits typically operate in siloes serving clients independently and competing for donors in the same geographic location. Many initiatives within population health models will require operational and philanthropic partnerships in order to be successful and to meet audacious goals. It will become increasingly important for the health care organization to develop internal partnerships between different clinical practices and services including specialty practices, outpatient care, emergency department, rehabilitation, etc. Many initiatives will also require external partners, which will require shifting the traditional view of other nonprofits as competitors and approaching them as true partners with a shared vision. External partnerships could include other hospitals and health care nonprofits including clinics and health centers along with non-health care organizations including community organizations (Salvation Army, food banks, etc.), educational organizations (early childhood centers, universities, etc.) and faith-based organizations. To expand the traditional concept even further, partners may also include government agencies, law enforcement and for-profit corporations with expertise or resources in a specific area. Partnerships should be based on a shared mission and aligned goals to address community needs. Levels of partnership include: grant-making capacity only, networking to share ideas and information, collaboration and sharing resources to enhance the other partner's capacity and a true alliance with shared goals and metrics. Along with the organization, the philanthropy office will need to determine how to align itself with other nonprofit development offices.

Since health care organizations are often one of the largest nonprofits in their community, hospitals can be seen as natural conveners for community partnerships around population health priorities. While the health care organization may serve as a catalyst to initiate collaboration, this doesn't necessarily mean they should lead the venture. Great care must be given to make these important and complex decisions at the onset regarding operational and philanthropic partnerships. For example:

· A *formalized alliance model* joins nonprofits to function seamlessly to solve identified problems with philanthropy driven to a neutral entity such as a community foundation. Fund development is on behalf of a neutral, shared, legal, funding entity to fund projects from all engaged community partners.

· A *funding model* places the hospital as the lead organization to design the innovative model as well as the funding entity that supports engagement from community partners similar to sub-grantors – meaning the health care organization's philanthropy organization would raise all the money and provide mini-grants to community organizations providing needed services.

· Another option is to maintain separate identities for each organization with clear, distinct objectives and programs provided by each entity to form a collaboration, with each organization maintaining separate fund development campaigns raising money for the projects under each particular nonprofit. For example, the health care organization would raise money for treatment, the neighborhood shelter would raise money to shelter the homeless, the school system would raise money to educate the community on nutrition, etc.

No matter what infrastructure is chosen, community partnerships will have challenges for the organization as well as for the philanthropy office. Before seeking partners, organizations need to have a clear understanding of the strengths and threats of partnerships and work through all steps. A few operational questions to assist in moving from competitors to partners include:

- · What services are needed to solve the identified problem?
- · What is the role and value of each organization?
- · What are the funding priorities for each nonprofit?
- · Is there agreement on the metrics, timeline and deliverables?
- · Do you have shared needs and/or shared population?
- · Is there benefit to working together and sharing resources?

There are also philanthropic questions to address prior to moving forward, including:

- · Who will approach which donors?
- · Which organization will manage each donor's relationship?
- · How will the collaborative and each individual nonprofit be represented?
- · Which nonprofit will communicate to each donor and how?
- · What information is shared with the donor?
- · Will nonprofits solicit together or independently by project, geography, etc.?
- · What nonprofit officially receives credit for accepting the gift?
- · Who is responsible for the stewardship reports?
- · Who will hold the money?

A lot of preparation needs to be done prior to implementation of a partnership at this magnitude.

DONOR ATTRACTION AND ALIGNMENT

Foundations are already shifting how they will approach funding population health. Many foundations require collaboration between nonprofits to apply for a grant while some even expand the requirements of partnerships to include non-traditional institutions such as banks and public transportation. The Rockefeller Foundation hosted a new report from the Organization for Economic Co-operation and Development on venture philanthropy which shows the movement of organizational foundations moving from single grants awarded to one institution to a systems level approach. Foundations also realize it takes longer than the current one-year norm to have transformative outcomes. The report reflects that foundations are changing their strategy from widespread to targeted, expanding the engagement period from one to multiple years and moving from single grantees to multiple partners with an emphasis on innovation, potential for results and scalability. Many foundations also expect to serve as a partner themselves by providing expertise and access to grant recipients.

Individual donors have also been attracted to elements of population health--even though it may not have been branded as such. What makes population health difficult to grasp for the health care institution makes it attractive for the donor. First and foremost, population health aligns with a patient-centered and donor-centered perspective. While there are donors who are committed to a single organization, most impact philanthropists care more about the cause, such as curing cancer, than a singular organization. Donors can see the advantages of investing in projects that involve multiple collaborators in the community. It is not a far leap for current health care donors interested in diabetes to understand the value of not only funding diabetic strips for those who can't afford them but also enabling education about food choices and access to supermarkets to improve a diabetic's life.

Community-wide funding opportunities can appear to be more urgent and significant when multiple agencies join together, and it can signal a potential higher rate of return on donor investment. Philanthropists are very savvy and understand one institution cannot independently solve the complexity of some health issues. Population health enables a holistic approach to health care problems and identifies that it necessitates attention to genetics, environment, society, etc. to truly make an impact on health outcomes. Under this umbrella, philanthropists can have a larger impact on the whole. Seed money for a health care organization's new, innovative models of care are ideal funding opportunities for philanthropists with expectations to provide transformational impact – results that are measurable and scalable not just within a specific organization but have the potential to have widespread impact. Population health holds the promise to provide these system level changes. Foundations and individual philanthropists are increasingly blazing new trails in funding models designed to yield social impact as well as a financial return on their investments.

Population health also provides unlimited opportunities for donors to fund projects at every interest level and every financial level such as providing start-up capital for new models of care, services and programs that are not covered by insurance and community programming extending outside the walls of the hospital. Some philanthropic priorities within population health will parallel the familiar

Population health enables a holistic approach to health care problems and identifies that it necessitates attention to genetics, environment, society, etc. to truly make an impact on health outcomes.

acute care scope currently supported by health care donors. Capital support may still be needed, as well, whether it is to purchase equipment, to build a new community health care clinic or to purchase a mobile mammography unit to make prevention and early detection more accessible. Smaller major gift and annual giving donors will necessitate the philanthropy organization to break down and explain complex population health initiatives to focus on smaller components of each initiative. Population health fund development efforts can also center around specific initiatives for populations, such as diabetes screening. Hospital-based philanthropy is already engaged in community initiatives that fit these strategies, but the context of population health as a core organizational priority reframes the importance.

149

AMY DORRILL, FAHP, CFRE

EXPANDING PHILANTHROPY'S REACH & IMPACT

Population health also has the opportunity to identify and engage new prospects to the health care organization. Approaches such as accountable care units within the hospital are anticipated to provide a better experience and satisfaction for the patient and family by enhancing care coordination from an interdisciplinary team and engaging the patient and family in the process. Better outcomes and satisfaction levels will help increase the pool of grateful patients. Other value-based models such as patient-centered medical home models can also build stronger relationships with grateful patients. Medical home models focus on the management of a specific health condition such as diabetes or cardiovascular care which are the same funding priorities most health care organizations currently hold. Population health can also attract new donors that currently support other community organizations focused on prevention, education, environment, etc. that are now introduced to the hospital through the partnership.

POPULATION HEALTH STEWARDSHIP

Stewardship efforts will also need to adjust to meet the needs of the donor and fit the project's timeline and goals. Today's donors want measurable results from their philanthropic investments, but transformational projects are often difficult to measure and report on in a short time period. Since the focus is on complex, system-level changes, population health initiatives will require a significant amount of time to show substantial outcomes. Donors will need to understand the time commitment of the project, so they are not surprised by the slowness of progress to the desirable outcomes. Frequent updates and activities that engage donors in first-hand accounts of project progress will make stewarding these gifts less taxing and more successful. The new model of care may also make it more difficult to determine exact outcomes of a singular initiative or organization when collaborations expand to multiple institutions. Stewardship reports will have to incorporate this new set of realities. Philanthropy professionals will need to help donors have a clear understanding of what ultimate success looks like as well as incremental success. A strength is that the health care organization will regularly monitor, evaluate and adjust each approach to report to insurers, and this information can be used to provide robust updates and engagement opportunities for donors. Philanthropy organizations will need to develop a lengthier stewardship plan for leadership donors that incorporates frequent interim objectives and progress reports. It is expected to take an average of five to ten years for population based initiatives to meet established objectives. With an elongated donor engagement period, there is an opportunity to engage and ask major donors for an additional gift when interim objectives are met or new opportunities arise.

CONCLUSION

While the shift in health care delivery models may seem daunting for health care organizations, foundations need only to remain donor-centric and true to their mission to find their relevancy in the population health space. There is an organizational need to understand the mechanics for population health; however, foundations have never (and should never) lead with a business strategy to inspire donors. The inspiration comes from the possibilities of what can be accomplished through a particular piece of equipment, a new procedure or an initiative led by the hospital no matter the payer mix or reimbursement structure. At the core, foundations provide opportunities for individuals to save lives and to make lives better. Population health, with a goal of improving health outcomes, provides such a platform; thus, it is fundable through private philanthropy at every giving level. Population health provides opportunities for donors to ensure not only that a mammogram is available to detect cancer and treatment is provided by specialists but also that care follows them home. Disease can change lives forever--not just for the time they are in the hospital. Now, hospitals are aligned to meet the holistic needs of an individual and support heath not just physically but also spiritually, mentally and emotionally. Foundations have the opportunity to strengthen existing internal partners and bring together communities as never before by linking health care services to other needs. You only need to talk to a family caregiver of an Alzheimer's patient to realize the impact of avoiding a trip to the emergency department due to the expertise of having access to a nurse navigator in the middle of the night. While this service does save the hospital money by avoiding readmission, it is a game changer for the patient and the family by providing peace of mind to the caregiver and by reducing anxiety and improving outcomes for the patient who can now remain in a safe, known environment at home rather than entering a stressful, unfamiliar hospital.

While population health is focused on a "population" impact, the most important impact is on the individual patient and the caregiver. The foundation will need to be engaged and understand the organization's population health strategy and objectives to translate this vision into a compelling opportunity to impact patients and communities.

References

1. Allen, P.M., et al, "Guide to Health Care Partnerships for Population Health Management and Value-based Care." American Hospital Association, July 2016. http://www.hpoe.org/Reports-HPOE/2016/guide-to-health-care-partnerships-pop-health.pdf.

2. American Hospital Association: "Managing Population Health: The Role of the Hospital." http://www.hpoe.org/Reports-HPOE/managing_population_health.pdf.

3. Centers for Medicaid and Medicare Services: "National Health Expenditure Projections 2016 – 2025." https://www.cms.gov/

Research-Statistics-Data-and-Systems/Statistics-Trends-and-Reports/ NationalHealthExpendData/Downloads/proj2016.pdf.

4. County Health Rankings. "Rankings Background." http://www. countyhealthrankings.org/about-project/rankings-background.

5. Hamza Hasan, "Population Health Managers, Meet the Three Patient Types Central to Your Success," Advisory Board (October 23, 2013).

6. Health Research & Education Trust: "A Playbook for Fostering Hospital-Community Partnerships to Build a Culture of Health." http:// www.hpoe.org/Reports-HPOE/2017/A-playbook-for-fostering-hospitalcommunity-partnerships.pdf.

7. Health Research & Educational Trust: "Approaches to Population Health in 2015: A National Survey of Hospitals." http://www.hpoe.org/Reports-HPOE/2015/PopHealthSurvey_FINAL_picture.pdf.

8. McGinnis, J. Michael, Pamela Williams-Russo, and James R. Knickman, "The Case for More Active Policy Attention to Health Promotions," Health Affairs 21:2 (2002):78-93.

9. McKesson Blog. "Overcoming Barriers for Success with Population Health Programs." http://www.mckesson.com/blog/achieving-roi-in-population-health-management/.

10. Milken Institute School of Public Health Blog. "What is Population Health." https://mha.gwu.edu/what-is-population-health/.

11. Nicholas Cericola, "Philanthropy: Your Untapped Resource for Financing Population Health," Advisory Board (June 27, 2016).

12. Prybil, Lawrence, et al, "Improving Community Health through Hospital – Public Health Collaboration," Commonwealth Center for Governance Studies," University of Kentucky College of Public Health, November 2014.

13. Risa Layizzo-Mourey, "Why Health, Poverty, and Community Development are Inseparable," Robert Wood Johnson Foundation, http:// www.rwjf.org/content/dam/farm/books/books/2012/rwjf401342.

CHAPTER 10

Building and Leveraging a High Performing Philanthropy Team

Susan Dolbert

The metaphor of work in a television station can be aptly applied to work in fund development. Our frontline philanthropic gift advisors represent the on-camera anchors who deliver the news. In development, these are our team members who ask for the gift. However, for a television station, as well as for a health care foundation or department of philanthropy, the organization cannot be successful without the efforts of every team member. The station manager, foundation president or department head is also not to be forgotten, as her leadership is essential for the success of the team.

In broadcasting, news cannot be delivered without great writers, editors, camera persons and others. In development, it is not possible to present a compelling opportunity for a prospect to invest in the health care mission without team members who work in donor relations, communications, prospect management and more.

While duties and responsibilities vary among the members of our development team, each member must be recognized as having equal value, and each team member should feel empowered, supported and respected.

A great leader generally accompanies a great and high performing team, so it is important to start with what a great leader should look like, specifically viewed through the lens of philanthropy. While it would be unlikely anyone who works in advancing philanthropy would disagree with the example above, it is still not easy to create and retain a collaborative and productive environment that results in a high performing team. That said, it can be done. It simply takes, as Jim Collins articulated so clearly in *Good to Great*, "getting the right people in the right seats on the bus."[1] But, even that is not enough. Organizations also need the right leader to create, coach and maintain a high performing team.

When trying to create a high performing team, the description from Jon R. Katzenbach and Douglas K. Smith's book, *The Wisdom of Teams: Creating the High-Performance Organization*, resonates with both team leaders and members: "A team is a small number of people with complementary skills who are committed in a common purpose, performance goals, and approach for which they hold themselves mutually accountable."[2] For those of us in health care philanthropy, the list should also include a commitment to mission.

But, why are teams preferable to individual performers? You have heard since childhood Aristotle's reflection, "The whole is greater than the sum of its parts." Teams add the element of synergy, a connection among individuals, that makes them better than they would be alone. What is significant about a great team is that each member (each part of the whole) is necessary to maximize team performance. Take away one or more of the members, and performance suffers. Great teams execute more quickly and make better decisions. Great teams are more creative, more productive and have greater morale. And, important for the workplace, high performing teams have more fun.

A great leader generally accompanies a great and high performing team, so it is important to start with what a great leader should look like, specifically viewed through the lens of philanthropy. It is helpful to consider those behaviors that define a great leader, rather than traits. While great leaders can come in all shapes, sizes and personality types, behaviors can be learned.

BEHAVIORS OF GREAT LEADERS

· *Mission-driven.* Leaders must be fully committed to the mission of the organization, or it will be impossible to inspire teams as well as donors.

· *Goal-oriented.* Great leaders keep the goals and approaches relevant and meaningful. If team members aren't clear on the what, why and how of their goals, it will be very difficult to stay focused and centered on where they need to go and how they can get there. Great leaders check-in regularly with each team member, reinforce what is going well and help individuals course correct where necessary. When a leader imparts confidence about where the team member is going and demonstrates support, the path to success becomes much clearer and feels much more achievable.

· *Consensus builder.* Team members perform best when they are involved in setting goals and priorities. Nothing moves an agenda forward faster than buy-in from people who participated in discussions leading to important decisions. A great leader ensures all voices are heard and respected and, when a decision is made, that each team member commits to the decision.

· *Culture creator.* Great leaders recognize the influence and impact they have on the culture of their team. Leadership change can change culture, often very quickly, and there are dozens of anecdotes about how the culture in the organization changed when a new foundation president, department director or hospital CEO came on board. It is incumbent upon leaders to recognize this and to create a mission-driven culture that is supportive of each team member --yet built on accountability. The goal of a leader should be to create a culture that makes team members want to jump out of bed to get to work in the morning, because they feel respected, productive and supported in an environment where they also have fun and laugh every day.

· *Intentional, active listener.* If you ask people what they need, and if you listen with intention, team members feel valued and empowered. It is essential that a team member feels heard. That only happens when the listener's focus is laser-focused on the conversation. An intentional, active listener asks questions and demonstrates understanding. This is the same behavior successful philanthropic gift advisors employ in their relationships with donors.

· *Trust builder.* Stephen M.R. Covey's impactful book, *The Speed of Trust*, reminds us a team operating with a high degree of trust produces results faster and makes the team more efficient. A great leader is able to accelerate creating a trusting culture. Covey's research shows high performing organizations have leaders who build trust quickly and are willing to give trust to team members early in the team's formation--even before it is earned.[3] Great leaders start with an assumption of trust in their team members.

· *Empowering.* Great leaders hire the best, smartest people they can and then get out of their way. Team members need to know their leader has confidence in their abilities and decision-making, yet also know the leader "has their back" if a decision doesn't have the hoped for outcome.

· *Inspiring.* Philanthropic gift advisors have difficult, stressful jobs. For us, it's not only the philanthropic goals we set for ourselves but also the knowledge that if we are not successful our health care organization will not be able to build new facilities, buy new equipment or provide needed training and education for caregivers. This reality of hospital philanthropy requires leaders to be inspirational to team members. Leaders must be enthusiastic, optimistic and appreciative of each team member's efforts and able to encourage both hard work and out-of-the-box thinking.

· *Advocates for team.* Great leaders ensure their team's efforts are recognized deeply and broadly by communicating openly and clearly throughout the organization. Very importantly, great leaders also make every effort to remove obstacles that might impede team success and open pathways to help the team achieve its goals.

· *Committed to professional development.* Great leaders take time and dedicate resources to professional development. They support and encourage team members to participate in professional organizations, present at professional meetings and move out of their comfort zones by participating in cross-training. Through a commitment to professional development, philanthropy professionals return to the workplace with a greater understanding of the work and a reaffirmed commitment to their role. As many of philanthropy professionals also have specialized skills, it is important to support and encourage opportunities for skill enhancement and growth.

· *Champion for team building.* Pausing our hectic daily routines to spend time together as a team is difficult, but essential, to the success of high performing teams. Team building can increase trust and collaboration throughout the entire team, as it increases understanding of our philanthropy colleagues. Team building helps leaders recognize the differences in work-styles among team members and informs how to work best with each colleagues.

· *Firm but kind.* While these appear to be traits or characteristics, they can also be part of our learned behaviors. Team members look to their leaders for direction as well as support. Great leaders are firm, in that they clearly articulate expectations, ensure team members embrace those expectations and address issues directly. But, they are also kind in how they offer feedback. If expectations are not met, great leaders are kind in helping the team member transition out of their position and examine future opportunities.

· *Fair and consistent.* The need for leaders to be fair and consistent generally evokes a response of, "Of course!" However, a consistent complaint is that leaders can be arbitrary in how they respond to questions or issues with individual staff members. Great leaders are always fair in their interactions with each staff member and always exhibit predictable behaviors. It should never be overhead that, "I don't want to bring this issue to my manager, because I'm not sure how she (or he) will react." Uncertainty is a real killer to a culture of trust and openness and can paralyze a team member's decision-making ability.

· *Models behaviors.* Team members are very aware of what their leader does and how their leader behaves in the workplace. Great leaders model the behaviors they expect from their team members. And, very importantly, the leader is also viewed as a member of the team, who jumps in to do whatever is required to support the team and work toward team goals. He/she knows there is no such thing as "not my job" and demonstrates a willingness to do real work. When a team member has success, the leader acknowledges the good work, with attribution to the worker, and not to herself. As team member personalities differ, that acknowledgment might be in a widely distributed email, in front of the entire team or simply in a quiet "thank you" as the leader stops by the team member's office to let her know the work was appreciated.

While a great leader does generally accompany a great team, it is no guarantee. A great team needs to be assembled with forethought— from designing job descriptions to composing interview questions that help the leader see what each person can bring to the team through his skill sets, talents, work style and personality. Great teams have well-documented characteristics.

· *Diverse.* Great teams are made up of people with wide-ranging skills, talents and personalities. Diverse team members each bring their own history, knowledge, background and experiences that result in the team being able to consider a wider range of options and accelerate decision making and execution. High performing teams are made up of members with specialized and complementary skills. While it may be more comfortable to work with team members "just like us," each member of a team should add value and contribute specific skills that not only can help the team achieve its goals but also make better and more complex decisions more quickly. Complementary skill sets also provide learning opportunities for team members who may be interested in building additional skills themselves.

· *Common purpose and goals.* Each team member should clearly understand the organization's purpose and its goals, as well as the specific goals of the team. Team goals should be formed collaboratively with the team, not by the leader alone, so agreement on the goals is understood. Goals should not be discussed at the beginning of the year and put away, but should be a part

161

of almost daily conversations. At a higher level, each member should also understand the organization's mission and be able to accept it as his own. Mission, purpose and goals should be the underpinnings of each team member's work.

· *Resolve conflicts early.* High performing teams are not afraid of conflict. They recognize conflict is the natural result of having a group with diverse skills, talents and personalities, and conflict can have creative, innovative results. High performing teams recognize conflict, manage it well and resolve their conflicts early. Early conflict resolution is important to high performing teams, because they are focused on the organization's mission, purpose and goals; and they are driven to achieve, and hopefully surpass, the goals of the group.

· *Candor and mutual respect.* These two characteristics must be discussed together. High performing teams are comfortable being direct in their communication with each other, exercising candor when necessary to advance the work toward their goals. However, it is essential the direct conversation be conducted by demonstrating mutual respect. Language is extremely important in this regard, and high performing team members are purposeful in their choice of language. Again, as high performing teams are guided by mission, purpose and goals, team members use candor to move their agenda forward as quickly and effectively as possible.

· *Collaborative and innovative.* Collaboration and innovation are being presented together, as collaboration is often the driver of innovation. When collaboration happens, new and different ideas are introduced which can lead to more innovative, out-of-the-box thinking. In philanthropy, goals cannot be achieved in isolation. Each philanthropy professional has an important role to play in securing philanthropic dollars to help achieve the goals of the organization. Collaboration is at the heart of everything. And, in the complex environments in which philanthropy professionals work, creativity and innovation are essential to making a difference for patients and caregivers.

· *Empowered.* Members of high performing teams feel empowered. They believe in themselves and their abilities to be important contributors to team goals. Their empowerment is fostered by their leader and reinforced by the candor and collaborative nature of their colleagues. It allows them to take informed risks as they stay on the path to achieving their goals.

· *Make no assumptions.* Successful members of high performing teams have learned to not make assumptions before they gather information and bring the appropriate team members together. Team members discuss the issue, the challenge or even strategy around a potential donor. High performers are informed. They read, research and engage in conversations and discussions before they act.

· *Focus on what she can control.* A team member can be quickly derailed from her focus on goals when she becomes distracted with something out of her, or the team's, control. It is an important lesson to learn. High performing team members don't take their eyes off the prize – meeting and even exceeding their goals.

Finding a great leader and building a great team does not ensure success or high performance in an office of philanthropy. Strong teams must not only be formed with intention but also keep intention alive after the team is working toward their goals. As successful, serial entrepreneur Chad Halvorson states, "Leaders who want to build strong teams operate in a systematic way and use a specific toolset to build, shape and grow their teams. This formula not only involves what they should say or do but also what they should avoid saying and doing. Strong leaders work backwards by envisioning the future before they deal with what's in front of them."[4]

Creating and leveraging a high performing team takes constant attention by each member. Committing to and regularly reviewing the behaviors discussed in this chapter can keep a high performing team on track and identify any issues early. A commitment to one another and to the team itself is essential for maximizing performance, as well.

Finally, never overlook some key essentials that contribute to leveraging a team's success:

· *Communication* is one of the most important behaviors to inculcate in the actions of both the leader and each team member. Communicating openly, both formally and informally, is part of the fabric of daily work life. Create an environment where messages are clear, questions are welcomed, rationale for decisions is understood and priorities and goals are willingly adopted by everyone. Every behavior and characteristic described above is impacted by how well the team communicates.

· *Support*—down, up and across—is essential to leverage performance is support. When someone on the team succeeds or fails, she needs to feel supported. This is particularly important when discussing failures. It is also important to remember a leader needs support from team members as well as team members needing support from their leader.

· *Trust* is incredibly important, especially in philanthropy. Trust is the very core of philanthropic work, particularly in health care. It is a non-starter if donors do not have trust in the philanthropy professionals who partner with them to match their passions with the needs of the hospital, or trust in the medical professionals who provide their care. The same could be said within a high performing team in philanthropy. Without trust, there is no shared commitment to mission, core values or goals — or even in the performance of daily work. And, once broken, trust is difficult to repair. Because of that, it is extremely important the team leader and the team not only commit to a high degree of trust but also monitor both themselves and others to ensure trust is not broken.

A discussion about teams cannot conclude without one of the essential characteristics that guarantees long-term high performance. That characteristic is a team that values humor, laughter and fun in the workplace. Working hard while having fun makes a very productive team where the members jump out of bed to get to work in the morning. The fact that a team laughs and has fun together is a sure sign of trust and respect. It cannot be overvalued.

Raising money for health care is extremely important work, as it allows medical professionals to continually improve the care of patients and families when they are most vulnerable. Philanthropy professionals must be part of high performing teams so the people, programs, tools and facilities so needed in today's hospitals are provided to them through the generosity of patients, families, friends, corporations and foundations. Understanding and committing to the behaviors and characteristics of high performing teams will allow our philanthropy professionals to focus on this important work, achieve great success and have fun doing so.

References

1. J.C. Collins, *Good to Great: Why Some Companies Make the Leap...and Others Don't* (New York, NY: Harper Business, 2001).

2. J.R. Katzenbach and D.K. Smith, *The Wisdom of Teams: Creating the High-Performance Organization* (New York, NY: Harper Collins, 2006).

3. Stephen M.R. Covey, *The Speed of Trust* (New York, NY: Simon & Schuster, 2006).

4. Chad Halvorson, "6 Keys to Developing a Top-Performing Team," Inc.com.

CHAPTER 11

Regionalization and Systemization in Health Care Philanthropy

Betsy Chapin Taylor, FAHP & Fred Najjar

It is undeniable mergers and acquisitions of health care organizations have greatly intensified. In fact, the American Hospital Association says merger and acquisition activity in terms of both the number of deals and number of hospitals has been on a steady increase since 2003.[1]. Today, more than 3,000 facilities are affiliated with a health care system.[2]

As consolidation and integration accelerate and financial pressure for all providers intensifies, many systems seek to leverage their size, talent, infrastructure, capabilities, knowledge, processes, buying power and other attributes to drive enhanced effectiveness and efficiency. Within this new mandate, the philanthropy organization's moment to take an expanded view of value creation has come.

DEFINITIONS:

Since several models exist to foster partnerships with donor investors, including independent foundations, closely-related foundations and internal philanthropy departments, these various organizational structures are referred to throughout this document as "philanthropy organizations" for convenience. To make the distinction between system-level efforts and those occurring at locally-based organizations, local efforts are referred to as "affiliates."

Systemization and regionalization of philanthropy organizations presents an opportunity to leverage the scope and strength of the larger organization to advance philanthropy as a core revenue resource to fund the strategic aspirations of supported health care organizations at the local and national level. However, building an expansive platform also ushers in organizational design, change management, culture and control issues.

THE BUSINESS RATIONALE FOR INTEGRATION

As organizations embark upon a regionalization or systemization journey, it is important to articulate the rationale for change and the anticipated benefits. Bringing clarity to why the organization would undergo change—and the effort and angst that can go with it—can help create the willingness for participation and urgency for timely execution.

Common reasons organizations consider integration include:

- strengthen fulfillment of the organizational mission
- increase total philanthropic dollars raised
- improve Return on Investment of fund development activities
- consolidate non-donor-facing activities (i.e. data management)
- share specialized talent and resources
- leverage human and budget resources
- capture a broader view of donor engagement
- share boundary-spanning funding opportunities

168

· drive standardization in development practice
· enhance the donor-centric experience
· diminish duplication and/or competition in donor engagement

Within these opportunities, one of the most powerful levers to enabling new levels of performance is to enable a programmatic pivot to intensify focus on high ROI activities. For example, with integration, the role of local affiliate organizations is often recast to place a primary focus on relationship-based, major and planned gift activities. This leverages the value of local presence to forge personal local relationships while realigning or centralizing a range of non-donor-facing activities. This also stems from clarity that the highest and best use of gift officer talent is in advancing relationships, so many organizations have sought to remove distractions and eliminate the "noise" that can undermine relationship work. At the same time, organizations going through integration have taken this opportunity to up the ante around data management efforts to support better use of analytics and better portfolio management processes. Many organizations also utilize integration to consolidate high value resources, such as planned giving expertise, into a single site or hubs to serve multiple locations rather than duplicating or underutilizing expensive expertise at local affiliates. Whatever path is pursued, it critical to be able to connect the dots between how realignment will improve or enhance the organization's capacity to raise more money more efficiently, since integration is a means to an end rather than an end itself.

CRAFTING STRATEGY

Based upon the strategy and structure variances across high performing organizations that have successfully implemented a systemization or regionalization strategy, it is clear there is no universal "right" path to integration. However, lessons learned from early movers provide valuable insights for those considering the journey. For example:

· great strategy is about optimizing value rather than creating complexity
· performance is driven by access to resources, expertise and capabilities
· excellence is achieved through attention to efficiency, effectiveness AND service
· strategy must be formulated and pursued within the context of culture

An early consideration is the scope of the integration ambition. Will the focus be to:

· Create a national-level, system structure to serve all regional and local affiliates?
· Unite local organizations sharing geographic proximity into regional structures?
· Align select organizations based upon unique characteristics or circumstances?
· Accomplish several of the above in sequence or at once?

As organizations formulate strategy, plans must consider both changeable and fixed organizational variables. These include:

· organizational culture to include the perception/prioritization of philanthropy
· use of regionalization/systemization in other organizational business units
· resolve and commitment of executive and philanthropy leadership
· geographic dispersion of entities involved
· existing leadership expertise and experience in philanthropy
· legal and governance structures of existing philanthropy organizations

· existing integration of system and market-based strategies
· unique founding stories, heritage and cultures of local affiliates

Finally, any proposed strategy needs to ensure the focus remains the focus: the philanthropy organization exists to foster meaningful partnerships with donors who are moved and motivated to make charitable investments in the health care organization's mission and vision of potential. Therefore, any strategy needs to hold relationships between the organization and donor investors as sacrosanct. New ambitions and operational structures must support a positive donor experience, maintain the integrity of personal relationships, foster ongoing engagement and allow excellent stewardship. Even knotty issues that arise such as shared prospects or donor engagement in multiple sites must be resolved with a donor's interests at the forefront.

DEFINING THE OPERATING MODEL

Organizations pursuing an integration strategy must be cognizant of "playing the game" on several interacting levels to consider and structure interplay between and roles of philanthropy leaders at local, regional and system levels. Integration also introduces new levels of complexity, with elements of work split across local, regional and system levels of the organization. This necessitates the thoughtful creation of an operating model that serves as a link between strategy and organizational design to deliver upon the strategy and to clarify how and where work will get done.

Organizations pursuing integration often confront the issue of deciding which activities should be centralized. Centralization adds value when it removes burdensome or distracting work from local affiliates, provides access to specialized expertise, fills gaps not being addressed at local sites, reduces cost or enables efficiency. However, centralization can also have clear downsides. It can make core processes more complex, add layers of red tape or delays to decision-making, remove work from those with local information or decrease ownership of the work product. Therefore, organizations building an operational framework must think through what critical work must be done and where it is best handled to enable efficiency, effectiveness and great service to donors. There is additional discussion about centralization later in this chapter.

The organizational operating model provides the structure to enable strategy implementation. Ultimately, the operating model answers the question of "who will be accountable for what and how will things work?" It should address structure, roles and processes in the most holistic way possible to determine how key responsibilities will be divided up across the organization. It should determine organizational layers, decision rights and lines of accountability. It should be designed to enable agile decision-making and to support innovation. It should also align with the organization's culture, values, vision and ambitions to advance meaningful philanthropy.

VOLUNTEER LEADERSHIP ENGAGEMENT

The integrated organization must also consider the roles, responsibilities, decision rights and engagement of foundation board or development council volunteer leaders.

A core question around community leadership volunteer engagement going forward is how much authority volunteer leaders have now. For example, is the philanthropy organization currently a department under the health care organization's 501(c)(3) status with a development council or other advisory body without legal governance responsibilities, or is the philanthropy organization a legally separate 501(c)(3) public charity or supporting organization with a true board of directors with legal obligations for providing governance? How will the organization be legally structured going forward, and what consequences will that have for board leadership? Board members deserve clarity around the new roles, responsibilities and expectations of membership and transparency around how future board engagement will be structured.

Navigating Variations in Legal Structure

As part of due diligence, the implementation path must consider the legal structure of existing philanthropy entities. Health care organizations currently utilize several legal structures to advance philanthropy work. Structures include:

- Philanthropy department: Uses health care organization 501(c)(3) status
- Foundation: Separate 501(c)(3) public charity
- Foundation: Affiliated 501(c)(3) supporting organization

Organizations have pursued different pathways to reconcile differing legal structures to create a common platform for advancing philanthropy.

- **Dissolve existing local structures to consolidate into a single regional and/or system-based structure(s)** The greatest benefit of consolidation is simplification of the business "back end" to streamline accounting, tax filings, insurance, governance structures and staffing structures. The most commonly noted detriment to consolidation has been the loss of local ownership for the entity to include a decrease in the engagement of community-based leaders.

- **Migrate all philanthropy organizations to a common legal structure** This accomplishes uniformity, but it is not without its own headaches as it often requires legal maneuvering, interaction with state-level regulators and sometimes the IRS. If organizations migrate to a single legal type, there is value to considering the context within which the philanthropy entities and supported health care organizations exist; for example, an organization that perceives itself as vulnerable to sale / merger may want to pursue utilization of separate 501(c)(3) entities to provide additional assurance to donors that all money will stay local regardless of future potential sales or affiliations. Alternatively, some organizations are willing to overlook potential future eventualities to maintain a tighter level of control today, so they may migrate to departments. It should be noted there is frankly limited utility to migrating all organizations to a single type of philanthropy entity; the value rarely justifies the effort.

- **Leave diverse legal structures intact** There are no fundamental differences between how philanthropy is advanced under each structure and, as noted above, the efficiency and benefit of uniformity is limited.

173

Sensitivity needs to be practiced in regard to the governance role, ownership and decision-making rights of the board of directors of a separate health care foundation. Community leadership volunteers serving in this capacity often feel a deep obligation to be proactive stewards of charitable assets and want to feel confident local charitable investments will be deployed to create local impact. Health care organizations that overlook or run roughshod over local foundation boards suffer a range of consequences from disenfranchising key board advocates to negatively impacting community ownership worse.

Board members deserve clarity around the new roles, responsibilities and expectations of membership and transparency around how future board engagement will be structured. Many integrated organizations retain volunteer structures organized to strictly serve at the local affiliate level; however, some organize regional level boards or bring representatives from affiliate-level volunteer leadership groups to participate on a representational "board of boards" at the system level to foster collaboration, communication and unity. Most systems have undertaken proactive efforts to enhance board member performance by providing system-sponsored board education to achieve a common platform of knowledge and expectations; education is delivered by system-level staff or external consultants. Several have created a single board member manual that is distributed to all local affiliate organizations.

Volunteer boards can be a valuable asset to philanthropy. As honest brokers serving to achieve a greater good, they have credibility that brings unique value to the enterprise and provides important connections to the local community. Since local board members may fear having their roles diminished by a system-level development function, it is crucial to maintain transparency as well as timely, meaningful communications to keep this group engaged and to ensure they feel a continued sense of ownership.

STRUCTURING PHILANTHROPY LEADERSHIP

Titling for the most senior system level executive for philanthropy must reflect consistency with each system's internal titling nomenclature for system-level senior executives. However, this title is recommended to be "senior vice president for philanthropy." Utilizing the SVP title aligns with typical titles at the top of most system organizations, since this role would be a peer to other system-level senior executives with a direct report to the system CEO. At the same time, using the SVP title eliminates confusion between the system role and regional or local affiliate level titles. Further, the title shifts from "development" to "philanthropy" to not only more accurately reflect the spirit and intention of the role but also to eliminate confusion with organizational development, business development and other similarly titled roles.

While there is variation amongst key roles and responsibilities for the SVP within existing systems, core responsibilities typically include:

- set an enterprise-wide vision and strategy for philanthropy
- align philanthropy with the health care organization strategic plan
- influence how talent and budget resources are best allocated across enterprise
- create system infrastructure and resources to elevate performance in all sites
- drive standardization of processes, data infrastructure and similar
- define metrics and drive accountability across the organization
- educate executives and board on strategic and financial value of philanthropy
- serve as the principal gift officer for the system
- select and mentor regional, and sometimes local, philanthropy executives
- provide connectivity between system vision and the local affiliate work
- foster a culture that understands, appreciates, supports and advances giving

· ensure a common vision, common knowledge and common best practice tools
· foster information-sharing, cross-pollination and collaboration across entire team
· ensure access to the best possible tools and resources to elevate practice
· serve as an internal consultant and coach for staff and boards
· manage system-level and regional-level philanthropy executives while also serving as a leader for all philanthropy professionals across the system

A regional vice president for philanthropy guides a regional hub for the organization. She would typically have a direct report to the SVP of philanthropy and a dotted reporting line to the regional CEO for the health care organization. This regional VP would have a variety of roles to include:

· cascade down and advance system-level strategy for philanthropy
· oversee centralized back-office and specialized services at regional hub
· influence or determine regional programmatic and funding priorities
· manage, mentor and coach local affiliate chief philanthropy officers in region
· serve as a resource and internal consultant to regional CEO and local boards

A chief philanthropy officer provides leadership at the local affiliate level. She has a direct reporting relationship to the regional vice president for philanthropy as well as dotted line reporting relationship to the local health care organization CEO. However, the system level executive retains authority as needed to hire, hold accountable or dismiss a local philanthropy executive. The local chief philanthropy officer is charged with leading local efforts to proactively foster relationships with well-qualified prospective donors, collaborate with the local CEO, manage and mentor the local philanthropy team, facilitate the involvement of physicians and clinicians and engage local volunteer board and council members as advocates and connectors.

Often, the organization will need to promote or seek leadership talent to fill some of these positions, and the goal should be to secure the best talent possible regardless of current or past affiliation with the organization. An open and fair process should also be used to actively seek internal and external candidates.

TALENT MANAGEMENT

Talent management is often a challenge in significant integration efforts. While the organization has a full bench of philanthropy professionals, that does not guarantee the organization has the right talent. For example, the organization must consider:

· What leadership roles will exist within the new operating model?
· What is the caliber and level of experience of existing philanthropy leaders?
· Are existing leaders capable of stepping up into regional or national roles? Do they have the knowledge and leadership skills? Do they have respect and credibility amongst their colleagues to assume a broader span of control?
· Will the evolution of the organization mean a different skill set or competency is needed now? Does the emerging organization have different needs and priorities to address? Does the realigned organization need someone to build upon existing successes or does it need a change agent who can effectively champion a new way of doing business?

Another consideration is around "dotted" versus "solid" reporting lines. Many local chief philanthropy officers already play for two coaches between the health care organization CEO and the foundation board or development council. Now, ushering in regional or system leadership means there is another strategic leader with a purview over the philanthropy function. This has led to consternation in many organizations over which lines of accountability are "dotted" with more informal collaboration and which lines are "solid" with true accountability. For example, some organizations say the local affiliate chief philanthropy officer should be a direct report to the health care organization CEO to ensure close collaboration, inclusion on the executive team and access to information and relationships; other organizations have found the local chief philanthropy officer should report to regional or system philanthropy executive who has deep understanding of fund development strategy and information to set appropriate goals and performance expectations. Making the correct decision on where ultimate accountability lies is both a strategic and cultural choice.

Integration also creates an ideal opportunity to create a common platform for the development and deployment of core philanthropy competencies throughout the organization. An enterprise-wide commitment to education can fill existing knowledge gaps and provide a platform for enhanced performance system-wide. Local affiliates who lack adequate budgets for continuing education wholeheartedly welcome this value-added service. This effort would disseminate a consistent body of knowledge across the system, support the sharing of best practices, facilitate networking among colleagues, build camaraderie and teamwork and conserve limited financial resources.

CENTRALIZED BACK-OFFICE, SUPPORT SERVICES

Some organizations pursue centralization of back office support services that are critical to success but that could be provided elsewhere. This includes ancillary functions - such as data management, financial and accounting services and vendor

Taking Best Advantage of Internal Talent

In large, diverse health systems, philanthropy talent and experience inevitably varies among individual hospitals. Integration provides a unique growth opportunity for skilled philanthropy leaders at the local or regional level to "spread their wings" and assume more responsibility within the system. This helps the organization retain and nurture valuable talent while enhancing foundation results throughout the enterprise.

selection - that support philanthropy but do not have direct interaction with donors. Benefits of centralizing non-donor-facing services include:

· achieving standardization of business practices across all entities
· removing high-volume or specialty work that could be done offsite
· hiring staff with specialization in functions that had previously been ancillary
· leveraging efficiencies of scale by managing niche services under a single effort.

Of all centralization opportunities, data management (which includes data entry, report writing, analytics, and process management) often emerges as the priority for several reasons:

· Data touches all aspects of the philanthropy organization. Creating a data-driven philanthropy organization is key to optimizing performance. Creating a robust, integrated, standardized approach to data can drive insights, target appeals, identify trends and enable performance evaluation.

· Data management systems are often the largest, single capital expense in a foundation office. Larger foundations sometimes fail to upgrade and smaller foundations often develop home-grown, spreadsheet-based systems in response to cost pressures rather than using the most effective tools available to store, utilize and analyze data. It sometimes takes prioritization of data management at the system level to enable the requisite investment in the best data management solution.

· For many organizations, standardization of donor data management is a necessary precursor to integration efforts. Achieving standardization of definitions and processes allows for collaboration and comparison that is otherwise challenging. Data integration and standardization also paves the way for process improvement.

Implementing system or regional level data management requires culture building and collaboration with the local affiliates first, since many can find data centralization threatening. However, it should be noted that implementation of a centralized data strategy is expensive not only in terms of procuring an enterprise-level database system but also in hiring, training and housing central office staff.

While barriers from start-up costs to initial resistance from local affiliates may pose challenges to pursuing centralization of non-donor facing activities, the projected benefits of centralizing back-office support functions almost always outweigh the costs.

CENTRALIZED PHILANTHROPY SERVICES

Centralization also occurs with specialized functions like planned giving, grants management, direct mail, communications or special events where practitioners with unique skills sets serve multiple sites as internal consultants. This not only leverages resources and expertise that might be otherwise unattainable by local affiliates or that does not necessarily need to be duplicated across every affiliate but also allows for spreading fixed costs across multiple sites.

Challenges to centralizing these types of tasks include initial local resistance over perceived loss of control, reduced personalization of some communications and decisions over cost allocations. Key benefits include realizing economies of scale, providing access to specialized expertise and developing internal consulting capabilities.

PERFORMANCE MANAGEMENT

Enterprise-wide performance management systems present both a significant opportunity and another area of complexity to navigate. Often, the emerging regional or system entity includes a collection of foundations with very different characteristics, levels of historical performance and even potential. For example, even a single geographic region could encompass philanthropy organizations that include rural facilities, mid-size community hospitals and academic medical centers. Some local affiliates focus almost solely on events while others have mature development programs with a strong major gift focus. Some have an executive who is simultaneously juggling management of the foundation, marketing, gift shop and volunteer services while another may have a deeply experienced philanthropy leader solely focused on philanthropy. Potential for significant variation in resources, talent, performance, culture, brand strength, leadership engagement, opportunity and more go on and on. This makes it challenging to calibrate appropriate accountability metrics that are applicable across the integrated organization.

Achieving a common understanding of what is counted and how is essential to enable both a common language and performance management.

The first step toward creating a regional or system approach to accountability sounds very pedestrian: get an accurate accounting

181

of all philanthropic dollars currently raised. While it seems obvious each local affiliate knows what they raise now, they often don't. Further, variation creeps in through many forms to cause a range of comparison issues early on. For example, FASB provides limited guidance on charitable revenue accounting, and their guidance can be interpreted differently from site to site. Some organizations count using GAAP accounting while others use the production accounting method common in the fund development field. Some accrue pledge commitments as receivables while others only count cash flow. Some count every gift at face value while others discount based on the time value of money or likelihood of default. Some are on one fiscal year while others embrace a different accounting period. Some count dollars within philanthropic production that aren't philanthropy but are transfers or pass-throughs from the health care organization or related entities like the volunteer Auxiliary; you also must grapple with if and how organizations count government grant contracts that provide income but are not philanthropy. All that said, don't underestimate how challenging it will be to get a correct baseline of financial information. Achieving a common understanding of what is counted and how is essential to enable both a common language and performance management.

Ultimately, the organization will want to move toward enterprise-wide benchmarking, evaluation and accountability. Ambitions include:

· standardize internal definitions and data management practices to allow apples-to-apples benchmarking and comparison of performance across system

· determine both financial and activity metrics for philanthropy

· recognize high performers to inform practice across all affiliates

· focus organizational attention on areas of practice that drive performance

· create organizational transparency to hardwire a culture of accountability

· set accurate system-level revenue goals

While the benefits of creating a culture of accountability to drive performance improvement are clear, there are also challenges to implementation, these include:

· determine financial and activity metrics meaningful to affiliates that vary in size, culture, program lifecycle, ally engagement, philanthropy talent and more

· overcome the fear and pushback of the region or system setting expectations

· recognize transparency of results embarrasses low performers in front of peers

· ensure data collection informs improvement rather than just being burdensome

· decide how to share credit for collaborative activities that benefit multiple sites

As the organization moves toward integrated performance management and accountability, it will be important to do so with a baseline of trust and respect already in place, because this starts to shine light where some organizations feel called out or embarrassed by the comparisons to benchmarks or their peers. However, this is a necessary part of moving toward excellence. Setting appropriate ambitions for evaluation will be dependent upon a thorough understanding of the current status of philanthropy from organization to organization across the system. Goals also need to be well-informed and genuinely attainable based upon the current realities in order to drive performance rather than despondency.

CHANGE AND CHALLENGE

While pursuing integration is desirable to some for the strategic opportunities it offers and will be compulsory for others because of overarching system plans, it must be noted that there are rampant tales of false steps and implosion risks to implementing a systemization or regionalization strategy. Simply, this is a complex and multi-dimensional ambition that must be supported by a well-informed plan, adequate resources to create infrastructure and leadership resolve to see implementation through. Leaders who have navigated this terrain call attention to the following risks:

· getting the philanthropy organization out of step with the health care organization

· pursuing implementation with inadequate commitment from system leadership

· adding unnecessary complexity to or overcentralizing key operational processes

· adding unneeded management layers that cause inertia, confusion and cost

· alienating or depleting the ownership of local executives, boards and councils

· underestimating how the skill sets of philanthropy leaders may need to adapt

· allowing ambiguity about plans and leadership roles to cause a talent exodus

· forgetting donor loyalty and relationship-based giving are local in nature, so every effort must be made to respect the interests and loyalties of donors

Challenges of integration extend well beyond strategy formulation and implementation. The human factor should not be overlooked. The prospect of integration can spark fear among detractors, create active resisters and alienate others who are not willing to change. There is often resistance to move from one world to a new one when few feel the existing one is broken. Thus, integration must be advanced with clear and consistent communication, transparency of purpose and sensitivity to those who will grieve or dig their heels in when facing change. There also needs to be assurance that integration efforts are not intended to "take away" but to add support.

There are prerequisite commitments and qualities that can smooth the path, such as:

· baseline of trust between all involved parties

· impetus for and shared vision for change
· collective approach to implementation
· clearly articulated steps along the change / integration journey
· transparent information on positive/negative implications of change
· understanding of each organization's commitment to achieve vision
· executive champion to keep all partners focused on shared agenda
· public commitments from organizational and/or regional CEO
· objective navigator to guide process – outside politics and impact

However, to strengthen your chance for a smooth implementation, an integration effort needs to be advanced with change management in mind. Key issues include moving from a singular to collective purpose, perception of inherent value delivered by the change, ownership of organizational vision and inevitable feelings of grief and loss associated with change. Open, honest, and frequent communications are a "must have" for an effective transition to take place. Organizations are cautioned about moving too quickly; situations must be nuanced through a careful appreciation and respect for local politics, personalities and cultures.

Above all, it is crucial for organizations to clearly articulate the rationale for integration to board and staff constituencies. Leaders must convincingly explain how the fulfillment of their charitable mission will be improved by virtue of the proposed changes. To satisfy the needs of community leadership volunteers, this justification generally needs to extend beyond the practicalities of dollars and cents.

CONCLUSION

Regionalization and systemization of health care philanthropy is not a one-size-fits-all endeavor. An understanding of local markets, entities, personalities and politics should factor into the decision on how, when and to what degree integration of strategies are developed and deployed. The benefits of structured collaboration need to be carefully examined and analyzed, as should associated risks and challenges.

After all issues are examined, most health systems will conclude there are real, tangible benefits for integration of part or all of their fund development efforts. It is a journey that may require some blood, sweat and maybe even a few tears...but the end result will be a stronger, more efficient and more effective philanthropy program for your organization...and better, safer and more accessible health care for the communities served.

Authors' Note:

The authors thank the many system philanthropy executives who generously shared insights, inspiration and cautionary tales to assist us with this effort, particularly those leaders who are part of the Health System Philanthropy Leadership Group. Additionally, Betsy sends special thanks to Philip H. McCorkle, Jr., for the privilege of three years around the table driving systemization efforts for Trinity Health.

References

1. American Hospital Association: "Trendwatch Chartbook 2016: Chart 2.9: Announced Hospital Mergers and Acquisitions, 1998 – 2015." http://www.aha.org/research/reports/tw/chartbook/2016/chart2-9.pdf.

2. American Hospital Association: "Trendwatch Chartbook 2016: Chart 2.4: Number of Hospitals in Health Systems, 2004 – 2014." http://www.aha.org/research/reports/tw/chartbook/2016/chart2-4.pdf.

Colophon

As the health care industry repositions from a reimbursement system based upon volume to one based upon value, the importance of philanthropy as an alternative revenue source has never been greater. Today's philanthropy organizations must intentionally pursue increased performance and greater efficiency to fulfill their mandate to power the health care organization's most important plans. Rising expectations demand a keen focus on values-based and relationship-driven partnerships with donors. Optimizing these partnerships is reliant upon understanding the power of gratitude as a motivator for giving, fostering the engagement of physicians and clinicians as true partners, infusing portfolio management with rigor and harnessing the power of both data and ongoing evaluation. Inspired and empowered teams of philanthropy professionals must also recalibrate the intent of annual giving programs, better integrate planned giving efforts and improve alignment between philanthropy and health care's emerging priorities. All of these issues and opportunities are confronted and explored within these pages by inspiring and challenging industry leaders.

Editor Betsy Chapin Taylor, FAHP, is a provocative industry thought leader who continues to push the health care philanthropy field to more vibrantly fulfill its mission. Her work has been featured by associations including the Association for Healthcare Philanthropy, American Hospital Association, American College of Healthcare Executives and in publications including Healthcare Executive, Trustee, BoardRoom Press, Becker's Hospital CFO Report, The Chronicle of Philanthropy, Chief Executive Officer, H&HN Daily, Healthcare Philanthropy and more. Taylor's previous books include Healthcare Philanthropy: Advance Charitable Giving to Your Organization's Mission and Redefining Healthcare Philanthropy.

The Association for Healthcare Philanthropy is an international professional organization dedicated exclusively to health care philanthropy professionals. AHP's 4,500 members represent more than 2,200 health care facilities around the world.

Made in the USA
San Bernardino, CA
14 July 2018